IN PRAISE OF JONI'S WORK

"Joni's training was an amazing experience. She is full of wisdom, and created a team and program that allows you to rediscover—or discover parts of yourself that you didn't even know were there. I highly recommend Joni and any program she is involved with."
~ **Nikki Davison,** founder of Blue Ripple Blends

"The first coaching session I had with Joni was the beginning of a life-changing shift in perspective and a profound mentorship that continues to this day. Joni's credentials speak for themselves, but there is something that runs much deeper. She embodies mindfulness in a manner that can be felt simply by being in her presence. Her teachings are genuine, deliberate, and impactful, and she has the ability to reach audiences across all ages and levels of understanding."
~ **Jana Reynolds,** founder of Haus of Being and The Momenta Moment

"Joni is kind, gentle, and provides a nonjudgmental, listening ear. She offers helpful insight and manageable feedback. She is also an intuitive yoga instructor and mindfulness facilitator."
~ **Jamie Demarco,** founder of Art in Motion physical therapy

"Joni was a breath of fresh air. Great interactions with our group."
"Great speaker and great content."
"Joni was very knowledgeable and she put together a great presentation."
"5 out of 5 stars on her talk. 100% recommend to business leaders."
"Joni was probably a top 5 speaker for me after 6 or 7 years. She was really awesome."
~ from **Vistage business leaders,** after Joni's workshop

"Amazing workshop, loved the focus on skills, practice, and how to integrate into daily living."
~ **healthcare professional** after Plugged into Mindfulness training

The Space to Choose

A Path to Life Mastery

Joni M. Staaf Stamford

Copyright © 2024 Joni Staaf Stamford
All rights reserved.
ISBN: 979-8-218-97444-2

DEDICATION

For my dad, Joe, who always believed in me, encouraged me, and reminded me that *this too shall pass*. Your silent strength is still with me, a reminder that challenges are fleeting and resilience is enduring. Imperfect yet undeniably loving, you exemplified the courage to embrace life's joys and trials alike.

I know you'd be smiling at me right now as you watch me write and build things using power tools. Thank you for helping shape me into the person I was meant to become.

CONTENTS

Introduction 1
Part One: Mindfulness 7
    The Three A's of Mindfulness 15
    How to Practice 25
    Meditation Techniques 29
    Mindfulness: The Practice and the Life Skill 51
Part Two: Discovery 53
    The Koshas 57
    Locus of Control 64
    Strengths-Based Mindset 66
    Intelligence 68
    Fear 73
    Finding Meaning 89
    Final Discovery Questions 101
Part Three: Care 103
    Attending to Your Physical Body 109
    Balancing Your Energy 117
    Supporting Your Mental and Emotional Wellness 129
    Cultivating Your Wisdom 141
    Nurturing Your Bliss 155
    Forming Good Habits 165
    Sample Self-Care Schedule 168
Part Four: Connection 173
    Technology as a Potential Roadblock 179
    Nonverbal Communication 181
    Emotional Connection 191

Words	197
Communication is Input and Output	201
Useful Connection Resources	211
Takeaways	213
Notes	215
Bibliography	219

ACKNOWLEDGEMENTS

Thank you to my dear friend and wise editor, Elizabeth Ann Poe, who spent countless hours poring over my book helping me to tighten and clarify the content. I appreciate your time, effort, and expertise so very much.

Thank you to my children, Mars and Joey, who inspire me to continually grow and be the best version of myself. Thank you to my husband, Brian, who encourages me, holds me tight when I'm overwhelmed, and is my forever love and tech support. Finally, thank you to my mom, who has shown me by example how to persevere no matter what life throws at you.

In compiling this work, I have endeavored to meticulously cite and acknowledge the contributions of individuals whose ideas and information have enriched its content. However, despite my best efforts, errors or oversights may have occurred. If any such discrepancies have inadvertently arisen, I humbly ask for forgiveness and extend my sincerest apologies to those affected. Your understanding and graciousness are greatly appreciated.

Introduction

There I was, on top of a mountain off Old Fall River Road, the Fall River Cirque Scoop, in Rocky Mountain National Park. When I was at the base of the mountain, it had been hot, bright, and sunny on that July day. I was in a tank top, applying sunscreen and drinking tons of water to quench the heat. But at the top of the mountain, a chill in the air brought a flurry of wet snowflakes; it felt like a different season in another world. How could both be happening at the same time? I was reminded that perspective is everything.

In that sleeting moment, I reached my arms wide, surrounded by, and feeling connected to the delicate yet incredibly resilient wildflowers surrounding me. How did they survive up here? Sunshine one minute, snow the next. In that pause, as I looked up to receive the summer snowflakes, I realized that this place was reflective of life. Bittersweet. There are times of amazing clear blue, sun-shining joy, and moments where cold tears cloud our inner sky for what seems like more than just a season of darkness. Yet it was on this unpredictable mountain that the most unique and beautiful flowers thrived. Could it be that their resilience was a result of the challenging climate? That their hardiness arose from their struggle for survival? Rather than experiencing what we might call post-traumatic stress, these wildflowers seemed to represent post-traumatic growth.

Post-traumatic growth is a positive psychological change that happens in some individuals after they experience a crisis or traumatic event. Individuals who experience this don't deny their distress, but instead, they feel it and overcome it with a greater understanding of themselves, others, and the world; they sometimes even emerge with a renewed vigor for life. This book is intended to provide the tools to help you move toward post-traumatic growth. I invite you to plant and cultivate its seeds within yourself.

On the mountain, I was struck with inspiration; my mind scrolled through my years of life struggles and through decades of studying and practicing yoga, mindfulness, Eastern philosophy, and positive psychology. I felt blessed, both by all the opportunities I've had and all the troubles I've survived. All of it has made me who I am and helped me experience profound growth. Life hasn't always been easy, and I realized my resilience — my capacity to recover quickly from difficulty and stress — was something I had learned, just as the wildflowers that sprinkled the landscape on this mountain seemed to have done. Standing there, I recalled a quote commonly attributed to Victor Frankl, a psychologist and Nazi prison camp survivor, about resilience, "Between stimulus and response, there is a space, and in that space is our power to choose our response. In our response lies our growth and our freedom."[1] *The Space to Choose*, the title of this book, was inspired by these words.

In truth, I have been writing *The Space to Choose*, little by little, for years. I've returned to it again and again. What I needed was a spark of inspiration and a framework to bring it all together. Whether it was that beautiful moment in Colorado, the fact that my kids were growing into adults, or that my business was growing to meet the mental health needs of those in my region that brought me clarity, I don't know. But I do know the perspectives and practices in this book have helped me skillfully stride through challenges in my life and emerge with a sense of calm focus and a path I can return to, where I feel I'm living with purpose, peace, and joy. I've learned how to heal from my past and how to continually practice healing after each painful life event. Students, clients, and workshop participants with whom I've worked over the past 20 years have experienced such growth as well.

By reading this book, you, too, are taking an active role in your overall well-being and the quality of your future. You are taking a step towards living the life you want by healing from chronic stress and overthinking. Anxiety, tension, depression, burnout, apathy, frustration, fatigue, headaches, restlessness, stomach disorders, worry, overwork, substance abuse, eating problems, sleep disturbances, chronic pain, and other persisting conditions can all be the result of chronic stress. If you've experienced any of these, this book and its guidance may help you. The practices and philosophy you will encounter can help you cope with symptoms, address the root cause, and help with the healing process. It won't be easy, but it will be worth it. You will not only learn a framework for self-study but also various ideas and techniques to help you cultivate the patience and strength to live the life you envision. What I offer is not just platitudes; it is information based on the science of stress and the researched benefits of mindfulness and other evidence-based concepts. (Of course, continue to follow your health practitioner's advice for any specific conditions.)

It is possible to learn how to take control of your life. The human condition is ever-changing, and we are all riding a wave, or a roller coaster, from birth until death. We can't change that, but we can learn how to respond to the ups and downs with greater skill and ease. To live skillfully is to create a sense of balance and equanimity amidst the deepest valleys and highest climbs.

To get there, we first need to heal. Heal from the physical, mental, and emotional pain we've all suffered. Heal from our own self-criticism and that of others. Heal from expectation and disappointment. While I'm not here to offer you medicine or wave a magic wand, I am here to help encourage you to open your eyes to a new way of looking at what healing means.

While a physical wound sometimes heals without even a scar, emotional healing is very different. It requires a *process of learning to accept and be comfortable with reality as it is, again and again*. It doesn't mean that past wrongs will be fixed. It doesn't mean that those who hurt you will apologize. It doesn't mean your past will change (it never will). It doesn't mean everything will go your way in the future. Life will not be sunshine and rainbows from here on out. Healing is learning to accept and be comfortable with reality as it is. You don't have to like it, and it doesn't mean that you will be complacent about taking action in the future. Once you start to accept reality as it is, you can learn to direct yourself where you want to go and feel a sense of equanimity along the way.

You might think you accept reality as it is, but consider how often you get frustrated by things outside of your control. Long lines in the grocery store. Traffic on your daily commute. Thunderstorms on the week you planned an outdoor vacation. A lost chance to purchase tickets to a sold-out show. A to-do list that leaves you feeling like there's not enough time. Memories of trauma/stress/mistakes creep into your mind, and you want to push them violently away. Or maybe you've pushed these painful memories so far down already that they only manifest as tightness in your shoulders or jaw. Constant thoughts run through your head, *I wish I would have... If only... I should have... I can't believe that happened... Why me ... What if...*

We have limited time here. Not just on the pages of this book but in life. We are all going to die. It's not a popular thing to discuss because no marketing solution will fix that fact. But it's the reality that we all need to get comfortable with. We are going to die. So, we need to be asking ourselves these questions:

- Am I present, engaged, and happy?

- Who am I? Do I present the same on the outside as I feel on the inside/am I authentic?

- Do I own my shortcomings without being overly critical? Am I taking good care of myself?

- Am I communicating the truth clearly to those closest to me, and am I listening to others' truth?

If you're not happy with your answers to these questions or if you don't have answers, it's important to face that fact and sit with the discomfort of it. Because there is no magic pill or quick fix, no special app, no artificial intelligence (AI)-assisted technology that will fix it. Quick fixes might be marketed to you, but there is no magic solution. Not for weight loss, not for health. Not for stress reduction or sleep. Not for finding purpose and meaning. Not for happiness. The effect of a quick fix is often temporary, sometimes with many vast side effects. Plus, if you're not addressing the root cause of a problem in your body and mind, you are not "curing it." To be healthy, calm, focused, and productive takes effort, but it doesn't have to feel impossible. The key to success is accepting that everything changes, and therefore, you must be willing to adapt and mindfully choose your actions in response. This is how to live skillfully, with intention and purpose. You can do it. And you must practice doing it again and again if you want the rest of your days to be filled with more ease, more love, and more clarity.

In Sanskrit, *punah punah* means again and again. It's used in the Bhagavad Gita when Krishna reminds Arjuna of the unending cycles that permeate our world and existence, patterns that never stop, and things outside of our control. Just as the seasons change from fall to winter, spring to summer, just as dawn rises into day, then fades into dusk and night, change happens again and again. Just as The Bible's Ecclesiastes chapter 3 reminds us, "to everything there is a season:" a time to break down and a time to build up, a time to weep, and a time to laugh. As it is with our own cycle, our own unconscious habits, and patterned ways of being, they happen over and over. It's why we encounter the same types of problems in life repeatedly.

Punah punah.

While we don't have control over the larger patterns of the universe, the earth, and those outside of us, the good news is that we can learn how to have control over ourselves. Punah punah, again and again, one step at a time. Remember that you are part of a cycle and that you are beautiful and perfect, just as you are. However, there's always room for growth. And growth is what this book is all about! While my take on the content is secular and based on best-practice research and over 20 years of experience, I also draw on a multitude of wisdom traditions to support my points. You'll see quotations and concepts from Christianity, Judaism, Buddhism, Hinduism, yoga, and other disciplines, as well as bits of science and psychology sprinkled throughout. Mindfulness and the other practices you'll read about here are woven through various cultural, spiritual, native, and psychological traditions. It is all about being present and clearing our minds for our life's work.

There are four parts in *The Space to Choose*:

Mindfulness. Part One focuses on how to strengthen your muscles of self-awareness through a mindfulness mindset and various practices. This helps begin the process of self-control or inner control.

Discovery. In Part Two, you'll learn about accepting your strengths and your negative patterns. You will also explore the questions: Who am I? What is most important to me? We can't experience transformation unless we first recognize all our greatness and our growth edges.

Care. Part Three emphasizes how to deeply care for yourself, mind, body, and spirit and how, in turn, this can help you care for others more effectively. This is an essential piece of the puzzle. We can't wait until we are drained before we practice self-care; it's a daily journey to fuel ourselves for the path ahead.

Connection. Part Four aims to strengthen your ability to communicate and connect with others. In our social media driven, technology-influenced culture, our connection to other human beings is sometimes superficial. Yet, part of overall health, wellness, and longevity practices revolve around deep, meaningful relationships with others. This section will help you gain clarity about creating fulfilling connections with others through more effective communication practices.

Understanding each of these four parts requires an openness to new perspectives and practices that might not always be comfortable. If you want to learn how to get unstuck, heal, and live toward your dreams, you'll have to learn to accept and live with discomfort and apply the appropriate concepts to your life again and again; otherwise, you'll fall right back into being dragged by life, instead of holding the reins.

> *We think that the point is to pass the test or overcome the problem, but the truth is that things don't really get solved. They come together and fall apart. Then, they come together again and fall apart again. It's just like that. The healing comes from letting there be room for all of this to happen: room for grief, for relief, for misery, for joy.*
> *~ Pema Chödrön* [2]

Punah punah. We must learn resilience in our way of being so we can better sit with the cycle and skillfully respond to it again and again. I call my four-part method for learning resilience action-oriented insight, and I offer it to you as a space to see yourself clearly, a way to know and care for yourself, and an opportunity to skillfully choose how you want to live your life.

Part One: Mindfulness

(Self-Awareness & Self-Control)

8 / The Space to Choose

Right now, for a moment, notice your body breathing. The sensations of the rib cage moving. Now, feel the breath inside your nose. Next, turn your focus to the throat. Do that again, pausing with each experience, breathing in and breathing out. Feel the ribcage or chest moving. Is there constant movement, or are there moments of stillness? Now, can you notice the flow of breath inside the nostrils? Focus on the sensations. Is there a difference between what the air feels like on the inhale as opposed to the exhale? Perhaps you might feel coolness or sharpness on the inhalation and softness or warmth with each exhalation. Notice if there is a sensation in your throat with each inhalation and exhalation.

Have you ever felt your breath in this way? It's what happens when you are paying attention. For just a moment, you weren't thinking of the past or the future. Hopefully, you weren't wondering if you were breathing correctly. You just experienced a moment of pure awareness or mindfulness. If you can allow yourself to focus just long enough to be an observer before your mind starts to ramble, judge, or create a story, you're in the present moment. That's what mindfulness is: an intentional state of being that requires objective awareness where you set aside judgment or opinion so you can see clearly *what is*.

What happens much of the time is that our minds tell us a story about what is happening. You may or may not even be aware of this. Usually, the story is so tightly woven with what you observe that you accept the ramblings of your mind as fact without considering that you are creating a distorted view of reality. In truth, we all have an inner narrator who is sometimes quite mean and often dramatic, bringing in past pain that is irrelevant to current circumstances. The inner narrator can be a saboteur, creating unnecessary problems or stress. This happens partly because we live in a fast-paced culture that doesn't value time for a pause, introspection, or true relaxation. Instead, we are valued for being busy and taking on more than we can handle until the primitive part of our brain starts to feel like we are under attack. This attack activates our fight or flight system, and we remain in this mode, constantly scanning our environment for danger. When our primitive brain (the amygdala) is in control, we are tense, emotionally reactive, and convinced that the world is out to get us. There's a metaphorical angry bear around every corner, ready to claw us to death. It's challenging to step back and be objective because that requires using our rational brain (the prefrontal cortex). We can only access the rational brain if we learn to calm our emotional reactivity (which is the brain's limbic system, of which the amygdala is a part).

In other words, your rambling mind and emotional reactivity aren't your fault. Having a rambling mind or exhibiting emotional reactivity doesn't mean you're a horrible person, immature, or self-centered. It means you're likely under chronic stress, and your primitive brain has taken charge of your life. You don't have any space to choose how you respond to your circumstances or the thoughts that ramble through your mind. You're stuck in a reactive state, just trying to survive.

The good news is that understanding and practicing mindfulness and breathing techniques can help you transition out of your primitive brain and out of chronic stress. Then, you can garner insight and ultimately be more skillful in life. Building greater self-awareness and self-control is the first step toward this change.

Ask yourself these questions daily:

- How am I in relationship with this moment? (Am I distracted, frustrated, agitated, restless, resistant, peaceful, accepting, or observing?)

- How am I in relationship with everything in my life: physically, mentally, emotionally, and spiritually? (What's going on with each of these layers of who I am?)

- Do I notice the constant stream of opinion and preference in my mind? If so, can I let some of it go? What happens if I do?

You might be wondering why we are supposed to let go of our judgment when we practice mindfulness. When you're in the role of observer, you are just noticing without getting hung up on all the reasons you like or don't like whatever you're noticing. Let's face it, we have opinions about everything. *I like chocolate ice cream, not vanilla. I like her boots. I don't like his tie. I didn't want it to rain today. This traffic is ruining my life. This line is too long and makes me angry. I don't want my spouse/my child/my friend to do that because I don't like it.* When you choose mindfulness as a state of mind, you are simply noticing what is. You're leaving your opinion out of it. This is not to say that it is wrong for you to like chocolate more than vanilla. It's about realizing how much your inner narrator clouds the simplicity and truth of any given moment with an opinion. You might find that it's not necessary to have an opinion about everything. You might even find it freeing to just notice what's going on in the present without trying to judge it or fix it. Consider adopting the phrase, "It is what it is." Because, in truth, much of life just is. And it's not going to change based on whether we like it or not. Therefore, practicing non-judgment is a step toward embodying equanimity: mental calmness and composure, regardless of circumstances. Mindfulness doesn't deny you the right to your opinion, to your likes and dislikes, but it will make you more aware of the fact that your opinion is separate from reality. Using this awareness, you can ultimately choose how you look at and experience something. And the way you choose quite often results in either your happiness or your misery.

A Zen story illustrates this point: Two traveling monks were walking along a river when they met a young woman. Wary of the current, she asked if they could carry her across. One of the monks hesitated, but the other hoisted her up onto his shoulders and carried her across. Once they reached the other side, he put her down. She thanked him and departed. As the monks continued on their journey, one of them was brooding and preoccupied. Finally, he spoke, "Brother, we are taught not to have any contact with women, but you picked that one up on your shoulders and carried her!" The other monk responded, "Brother, I put her down on the other side of the river. Why are you still carrying her?"[3]

What do we mentally carry with us and bring to future situations? Are we carrying our resentment and judgment, our fear and our worry, and our disappointments about things not happening the way we think they should?

I understand; I've been there. It's difficult to be in the present moment when you're not getting what you want or what you expected. We all have conscious and unconscious expectations about everything from the weather, based on what a meteorologist predicted, to the behavior of our significant other, based on what we want them to do or not do; to travel, based on our desire to arrive at a destination without delay, just as we thought. These are everyday circumstances where we might experience frustration, stress, and even anger because things didn't unfold as we expected. It's even more challenging to practice mindfulness when we are experiencing deeper pain, grief, confusion, or loss. Instead, we crave distraction so that we don't have to sit in the metaphorical fire and face the burning of a painful present moment. While healthy distractions might sometimes be necessary, it is also necessary to face our circumstances and see reality clearly. In doing so, we allow ourselves to feel what we feel and acknowledge when something is outside of our control.

The choice to be present and accept pain is often impossible to make without training or support to guide us in the direction of this kind of present-moment awareness. Rather than embrace present-moment awareness, it is easier to fall into the autopilot of distraction and mindless (and sometimes unhealthy) self-soothing. This is why we have a skyrocketing substance abuse problem in the United States. It's why we have technology addiction. It is why mental health is declining, and suicide rates and shootings are higher than ever. As a Western society, we don't have many programs in place to help us learn how to manage stress, emotionally regulate, or even focus our minds. We are encouraged to blame others, distract ourselves, and live in a fantasy world. We get sucked into negativity and the misperception that if we can control, change, or even harm another person, then we will be happy.

As mindfulness teacher Pema Chödrön says, "There is no escape."[4] What she means is there's no escaping reality. There's no escaping pain. There's no escaping yourself and your own patterns without awareness and desire to step outside your mental spiral and habitual patterns of distraction. But if you learn to practice mindfulness, you can approach life in a new way. It's about taking personal responsibility for where you are, without harsh self-judgment (or judgment of others), and choosing to cultivate a better tomorrow through your best effort. This means acknowledging if you're in a constant state of distraction or negativity or if you realize you follow the stories in your mind more often than you see reality clearly. We all have our patterns. Mindfulness helps us wake up to them and eventually choose more skillful actions in the future.

14 / The Space to Choose

The Three A's of Mindfulness

When I first began working with CEOs, teaching them the importance of mindfulness, both as a practice and a discipline to live by, I received pushback in the form of comments like, "Joni, I don't want to get soft. Relaxing is great, but I don't want to sit in a cave and 'Om' the rest of my life. I need to be mentally sharp and get things done."

A common misconception about mindfulness and meditation is that their purpose is to make you relaxed and detached to the point of complacency. This is simply not accurate. To counter this inaccuracy, I have developed a way to clearly explain mindfulness and how it can offer you deep insight into yourself and your circumstances so you may make the best choices possible. This is the core of my work, and it's called action-oriented insight. It begins with the three A's of mindfulness, a framework I use in my own life, and what I've taught to individuals and those in my training programs for decades. The three A's of mindfulness are Awareness, Acceptance, and Action (skilled action).

Awareness

I get distracted by what
the outer eyes see,
by what the trickster in my mind
reads to me.
~ *excerpt from my poem, "Remember"* [5]

Cultivating awareness, the first A of mindfulness, is about learning to pay attention. You might be good at noticing other people's issues, what they need to change, or how they could fix their problems. Maybe you're good at analyzing situations, seeing the positives and the negatives, and making lists. While some of this involves awareness, it also involves layers of judgment and opinion. The "trickster" in our minds frequently pulls us out of a state of awareness and into a state of distraction, with sometimes fear-based thoughts or sometimes just rambling thoughts.

Pure awareness is about noticing, in as simple a way as possible, both what you see with your outer eyes and, more importantly, what you notice with your inner eyes. Awareness is the noticing that happens *before* you add your commentary. Most importantly, mindful awareness is about paying attention to your physical, mental, and emotional reactions to what's happening around you. It's a matter of making note, as objectively as possible, of what is in front of you, then honestly assessing your internal reaction to it:

- How does my body feel? (Does this make me tense? Am I clenching my jaw when facing this circumstance? Is my stomach upset? Psychosomatic reactions are natural and happen to most of us quite often, whether we are aware of them or not.)

- What emotions are present? (What's my mood? It's important to own how you feel. There's no right or wrong way to feel, but we need to see and own our feelings with clarity ("I feel sad," "I feel frustrated," etc.), before taking action.)

- What is the story in my mind? (Where are my thoughts taking me? To past stories and circumstances? To a story inciting fears regarding the future?)

Notice what's going on without telling yourself what you're "supposed to" feel or how it "should" be. Awareness is about strengthening your muscles of observation. Remember, try to minimize the commentary about what you observe. Catch yourself in judgment and try to shift to "just the facts." Learning to pay attention in this way is very powerful! It will take time, but it is worth the effort. Practicing awareness can help you steady your mind and emotions so you feel more in control.

Here's an example of a thought process not grounded in awareness, as opposed to one that is:

My best friend is going to be mugged. I'm sure of it! She's going to Paris alone. I don't know why she is doing it, maybe she's mad at me because she didn't ask me to join her, she does stuff like this and bad things can happen, and I don't know why she doesn't think about that. I try to tell her, but she doesn't listen to me. I know I'm right.

And now, practicing awareness:

My best friend is going to Paris. I notice that I'm feeling worried (anxious) and left out.

Practicing awareness will eventually enable you to observe accurately and regulate your feelings and internal reactions. The goal is to choose the best response to a circumstance rather than have a knee-jerk reaction (even if that reaction is just a rambling narrative in your mind). You will feel more calm inside if you just observe and release or at least edit the internal narrative. You'll be living in the present moment instead of inside your head.

Awareness is also about uni-tasking, as opposed to multi-tasking. Our culture urges us to do more, to produce more, to go, go, go. To be mindful, we must learn that we can only pay attention to one thing at a time. You can't scroll through your phone and effectively have a conversation with someone. You can't respond to emails and be present during that Zoom meeting. You can't cook dinner, listen to a podcast, and be present with your loved ones all at the same time. And you certainly can't enjoy a nature walk if you're on your phone or stuck in the narrative inside your head. This is a tough one, but try to notice your urge to multitask and instead just focus on one thing at a time. It will take a while to retrain your brain and learn how to focus, but your stress level will decrease, and your level of presence and appreciation for life will increase exponentially. And contrary to popular belief, you'll be more effective and get more done when you stop multitasking and start uni-tasking.

Acceptance

Acceptance, the second A of mindfulness, goes hand in hand with awareness, and yet it is a challenging concept to practice. When I've introduced or even said the word acceptance to a group, I've watched people visibly tense up or even shake their heads no. I've heard, "I'm not going to accept something I don't want or don't like. That's ridiculous!"

Let me be clear on our working definition of acceptance. Acceptance is seeing reality clearly, without sweeping anything under the rug, without saying to yourself, *I don't want it to be this way.* It's simply looking at the raw truth and saying to yourself, *Yep, this is reality right now. Yep, this is how I am reacting to it internally.* The truth is acceptance doesn't mean you have to like what's happening, you don't have to agree with it, and it doesn't have to be comfortable. It also doesn't mean that you are going to be complacent or that you aren't going to try to change reality if it is something within your control. But you do have to see clearly and sit with it first before taking action; otherwise, action is reactive instead of responsive.

Accepting reality involves practicing beginner's mind. To use beginner's mind, you practice looking at circumstances, as well as your internal thoughts and feelings with curiosity (*Hmm. . .isn't that interesting. I see what happened, and I can notice my feelings of anger.*) as opposed to opinionated judgment (*That did not just happen. I hate this; everything is ruined now*). That switch in perspective might seem challenging, but it allows life to happen; it allows space for you to experience life fully rather than being in denial or getting stuck in an explosive emotional reaction. It's about surrendering to what you don't have control over. Don't think of surrender as defeat, but as knowing that you've done what you can do, and the rest is up to someone else or the universe/God.

The following two philosophies can help you remember what acceptance is and why it's important. They are saying the same thing despite coming from very different traditions.

The Five Remembrances

This is a piece of Buddhist psychology that involves accepting these five facts about being human.

1. I am of the nature to grow old. There is no way to escape growing old.

2. I am of the nature to have ill health. There is no way to escape ill health.

3. I am of the nature to die. There is no way to escape death.

4. All that is dear to me and everyone I love is of the nature to change. There is no way to escape being separated from them.

5. My actions are my only true belongings. I cannot escape the consequences of my actions. My actions are the ground upon which I stand.

In other words, we must accept these facts of life and learn to find ways to manage the challenging emotions that accompany them because they are beyond our control. I recommend sitting with each of the remembrances and noticing any internal resistance. I realize that they sound grim and perhaps even overwhelming. However, there's a valuable growth opportunity in each one. I know for me, I always thought I'd skip the second remembrance, "I am of the nature to have ill health." As a lifelong healthy eater, exerciser, and meditator, I have always felt confident in my ability to be healthy and strong. That is until I wound up in the emergency room at age 42 with a pain in my chest.

"We found that you have an elevated enzyme in your blood that could be indicative of a heart attack," said the attending physician calmly.

"No, no, no," I said. "I have perfect cholesterol and low blood pressure; I eat right, exercise, and manage stress. I'm not having a heart issue. I think it's just bronchitis." I didn't want to see reality clearly.

Nevertheless, I had to check into the hospital and undergo an EKG, heart catheterization, and numerous other tests. All the while, I was either in denial or I was furious at my body for betraying me. At one point, I was crying hysterically to my boyfriend at the time, who was sitting at my bedside. Suddenly, I recalled the Five Remembrances. My hysterics immediately stopped. I was able to regain the rational self-control in which I had trained myself. "I am of the nature to have ill health. There is no way to escape ill health." I said it out loud. I realized that whatever the outcome of the tests, I would have to accept reality as it is and move forward as skillfully as I could. My actions are my only true belongings. In this scenario, I was blessed enough to recover completely from a case of myocarditis (heart inflammation), and I am my healthy self again, with full respect for honoring the uncertainty of life.

You can work with the Five Remembrances yourself to help you navigate challenging circumstances and emotions as they arise.

There's another piece of philosophy that says the same thing but with different words.

The Serenity Prayer

This portion of a Christian prayer conveys the same philosophical message as the Five Remembrances but with different words:

> God, grant me the serenity to accept the things I cannot change,
> Courage to change the things I can,
> And the wisdom to know the difference.[6]

While The Five Remembrances are direct and The Serenity Prayer more subtle, both call us to take skilled action. Learning awareness and cultivating a steady mind and heart will help you see life with greater clarity. This clarity can empower you to move forward, moment by moment, choosing your best course of action.

Acceptance allows space for all life experiences to happen: it allows space for pain, shame, sadness, fear, insecurity, and anger, as well as gratitude, joy, trust, peace, and love. It all exists as part of the human experience. The sooner we can wake up from the illusion of "as soon as I …(get that job, lose ten pounds, have a baby, get married) … then I will be happy," the better. Life contains both pleasant and unpleasant experiences. We shouldn't wallow in the difficult times any more than we should cling to the wonderful times. Awareness and acceptance are both practices to help you be fully present and engaged with the bitter and the sweet of life. When you're experiencing grief and sorrow over a loss, let yourself feel it. In your mind, say, "I am so sad over this loss." Mindfulness practice is about getting comfortable with the uncomfortable, sitting with your own pain, and knowing that it will pass, as all things do. More about how to practice this later.

Action

Action, or more aptly, "skilled" action, is the third A in the three A's of mindfulness. It is about being skilled in the steps you take to move forward. The best way to do that is to ask yourself, "Do I have control over this situation?" If the answer is yes, then plan out what to do and when or how to do it. That's taking skilled action. Sometimes, the answer might fall into a gray area; you might have some influence over the circumstance at hand. If so, consider what you have control over, remembering that you cannot control another human's thoughts, feelings, or actions. Sometimes, the hard reality is that you have no control over a particular circumstance, or you've already done all you can. So, when you ask yourself, do I have control over this? The honest answer is no. In this case, the skilled action is to move back into the practice of acceptance and find healthy ways to cope (meditate) with the mental and emotional turmoil that sometimes arises when life is not unfolding as you wish.

This third step of a mindfulness mindset is the most challenging. It requires not only the ability to self-reflect and take personal responsibility but also the ability to emotionally regulate. It means seeing and sitting with a reality that could be unexpected and painful. Putting a hard stop to any knee-jerk reactivity requires patience and lots of practice.

The following story from ancient Hindu mythology demonstrates overcoming knee-jerk, autopilot reactions and taking skilled action. First, it helps to understand three qualities that we all have within (referred to as the *gunas* in the Bhagavad Gita):

- *Sattva* refers to an inspired idea or vision. It is also the state of being in harmony.

- *Rajas* refers to the quality of action, be it a frantic, overreaction, or a more skilled action.

- *Tamas* refers to an obstacle or being stuck in inaction; we are in this state when overthinking.

The story begins with Ganesh and his brother Skanda. Ganesh is depicted as a slow-moving, elephant-headed boy. Skanda is a strong, athletic warrior. Their parents, Shiva and Parvati, challenge them to a contest, "Whoever wins, wins success and prosperity."

The contest was to lap the universe three times and return to the spot where they stood. Whoever completed their laps first would win. Without another thought, Skanda, the athlete, took off to run around the universe. Ganesh sat, feeling stuck and sorry for himself, thinking, *thanks, Mom and Dad, there's no way I can win this.*

While Ganesh sat, pouting, Skanda had already made one lap around the universe. After some time, Ganesh began to settle his mind and had an inspiring idea. He looked up at his parents and thought, *my parents are the embodiment of the masculine and feminine divine, and my parents taught me everything I know. To me, my parents are the universe.* Yet still, Ganesh did not move. Although he had a vision of the answer, he was in a state of inaction.

Then Skanda zoomed by, having made his second lap around the universe. Only one more to go. Ganesh decided that he had to take action. He stood up, walked around his parents three times, and stopped, looking up at them. They declared him the winner.

When we contemplate this story, it is important to acknowledge that the three gunas, or qualities mentioned above, are present within each of us. The quality of acting without thought (rajas), which Skanda embodied, caused him to expend a lot more energy than he needed to, and he still didn't win. The other side is Ganesh, who initially took no action and was stuck in the obstacle of the situation (tamas). After sitting long enough to center himself, Ganesh came up with an inspired idea (sattva), but he ultimately had to take skilled action by getting up and moving, for it to impact him. When he acknowledged and utilized all three qualities skillfully, he won.

You will encounter all three gunas. You will get stuck in both rajas (action) and tamas (inaction), so it's important to remember how they work together. You will always have obstacles to overcome. And so, you must cultivate self-awareness and self-control by calming yourself long enough to see clearly (sattva), and then, most importantly, you have to take skilled action.

Practicing skilled action will save you from the shame and regret that comes from having an overly emotional, knee-jerk reaction. We've all been there, either internally or externally, accelerating from 0 to 60 in a few seconds when something or someone pushes our buttons. When you're in that state, you feel like you're being attacked by a bear, and you must respond with the same ferocity. However, it's usually not a bear you're facing but rather your own fear and insecurity. Remember, your primitive brain wants to protect you at all costs, whether it's from a physical threat or what feels even more deadly at times, a mental and emotional threat.

So, how can you overcome the instincts of your primitive brain? With daily practice and specialized techniques. The first time you try to use the concepts of awareness, acceptance, and skilled action, it's unlikely you'll be able to implement them perfectly. You certainly won't if you are in a big trigger situation, with your family or spouse, with a big work project you're highly invested in, or if someone delivers a low blow regarding something you're particularly sensitive about. This is why we have techniques, and this is why daily practice of mindfulness is so necessary. Daily practice of mindfulness and the implementation of mindfulness techniques can gradually help you transform your primitive brain. In fact, there's research that shows a daily practice of mindfulness increases gray matter in the executive functioning region, as well as the memory center in the brain, while decreasing gray matter in the amygdala (freak-out center of the brain).[7]

Regular practice makes it easier for you to implement the mindfulness mindset of awareness, acceptance, and skilled action. We have to practice and allow our brains to catch up to the reality that not everything is a vicious attack directed at us. Only then can we flow through life with greater ease and less resistance to its inevitable ups and downs. This process is the essence of resilience, and it's the only real antidote to stress.

How to Practice

Forming a New Habit

Learning something intellectually can offer a new perspective and provide a catalyst for creating real change. However, intellectual understanding alone is not enough. Merely understanding the concepts of awareness, acceptance, and how to take skilled action will not change your brain's wiring any more than understanding the rules of soccer will make you a good soccer player. You have to practice.

There are two ways to practice, and both are valuable and necessary: informal practice and formal practice. Informal practice is when you take the concepts of mindfulness and try to apply them skillfully to your life in the moment. It's easiest to start in simple circumstances. In other words, start by trying to accept the weather for what it is without complaining (let go of your opinion about it and just be skilled in how you dress or whether you carry an umbrella). Don't, however, expect yourself to go to your next family gathering and behave like a Zen monk. You might be setting yourself up for disappointment and self-criticism.

Or you might practice informally in a familiar place like the grocery store. Imagine you're in the store to pick up a few things, and you're running late. Feeling frantic, you round the corner and are faced with multiple long lines. Notice the situation and inquire inwardly: *Am I frustrated, and do I feel a bit like throwing a temper tantrum (even if it's only in my head)? Do I once again wonder why the world is against me? Do I check out mentally by zoning out on my phone while I stand in line?*

What does practicing awareness, acceptance, and skilled action look like in this scenario? I have learned how to notice internal agitation and then let it go because I don't like how it feels, and it is a circumstance I have no control over. I have also found joy in simple little present moments, where instead of disengaging on my phone, I take the opportunity to focus on my breathing or look around and observe people and things around me. Sometimes, I'll even strike up a conversation with the person in line next to me. Life offers us an abundance of circumstances where we can practice being more present, patient, and less judgmental. Simply try to observe your opinion and let reality be what it is without resistance.

You can also choose to practice mindfulness informally when you're doing chores. Sometimes, this is when we multitask: we talk on the phone or listen to a podcast while folding laundry or doing dishes. While there's nothing wrong with that, sometimes, you can choose to make a chore a mindfulness practice by simply focusing on one thing. For instance, when you take a load of towels out of the dryer, what do they feel like? Have you ever been present enough to notice? Try focusing on the warmth, the softness, and the smell of freshly dried laundry. Doesn't that sound pleasant? You might feel silly standing at the dryer clasping a warm towel, inhaling like you're in a fabric softener advertisement, but what's the alternative? To miss that moment of your life? To miss the simple, sweet sensation of warm water and bubbles in a sink full of dishes, to miss the genuine smile on a loved one's face because you were on your phone, to miss the sound of bugs and birds on an evening walk?

Informal mindfulness is simply practicing greater presence in more moments of your life. It is being fully present, without distractions from inside your mind or from the urge to multi-task. It's about enjoying the moments you have while you still have them. The more you practice this as a habit, the more pleasant and effortless it becomes.

Formal mindfulness is meditation, a practice you regularly do to garner insight and center the nervous system. Formal practice is important and makes informal practice easier. First, you'll choose a technique (I'll introduce you to several), then you'll take time to practice it. Practice is necessary, just as if you were learning piano or how to play tennis; meditation is a skill that doesn't necessarily come naturally.

Committing to any new practice is challenging because it involves creating a new habit. Whole books are written on how to change habits, whether you want to eliminate a destructive one or start a healthy one. When we change our auto-pilot behavior, we rewire the brain and create new neural pathways, and that takes work. I equate it to the difference between walking through the woods on a paved path and hacking your way through thick brush with a machete. Eventually, with the machete (new habit), you will create a comfortable path, and it might even be paved so that it's easy for you to walk on in the future. But it takes work, discipline, and focus to form a new habit or create a new neural pathway. Intellectual understanding can support this endeavor if we allow it. If we know something will benefit us but we never do it, that could result in a negative spiral of thoughts where we criticize ourselves for not choosing better. But if we understand how something can help us and we take skilled action, little by little, we can form new habits.

Mahatma Gandhi famously said, "Happiness is when what we think, what we say, and what we do are all in harmony." Think about this the next time you say that you know you should be eating better, exercising, or doing something else that is good for you. Why are you choosing not to take action on it? What is holding you back? Some might say it's not that easy. Why not? Who is in control of your actions if not you?

Yes, forming new habits takes hard work and discipline, and that can be challenging to implement amidst an already busy life filled with other habits. This is when you need *tapas*. I'm not referring to an appetizer-type meal. Ancient Indian texts mention the word tapas, referring to the high degree of self-discipline required when you want high-growth rewards. Tapas is the inner fire and drive that helps you overcome your auto-pilot. It's the part of you that says yes to stepping outside of your comfort zone, and it's what will help you choose the life you want and how you want to show up in it. The Bible mentions its own version of tapas in Galatians 5:22, calling temperance or self-control one of the nine fruits of the spirit. The Islamic faith also values the importance of discipline and self-control. Even Western psychological theories like cognitive behavioral therapy are based on the premise that with training and practice, you can control your thoughts and, ultimately, your emotions and behavior if you practice. As you make your way through this book, you'll find many practices that will help you discover yourself, care for yourself, and connect more deeply with others in your life, and tapas or temperance is what's required for all of this. If you want to live the life you desire, you need to practice facing the fire of discipline.

You've got to start somewhere. If you want to commit to a formal practice of mindfulness, I recommend making it as easy as possible for yourself. Plan to set aside time in the day to practice, be it in the morning, at noon, after work, or in the evening before bed. Choose a place in your home that is visible from other areas you use. In other words, don't make your practice space in some corner bedroom that you never even walk by. Make it a space that you will notice by placing a cushion or putting a little seat near your bedside or in a room that you frequent in your daily routine. You might want to set alarms on your phone to remind you, write the benefits on a piece of paper and post it on your bathroom mirror, or connect this new habit of mindfulness meditation to something that you already do regularly, like brushing your teeth. That way, the next time you brush your teeth, you'll be reminded to also sit for five minutes. If you are motivated by a rewards system, try that. Perhaps splurge on a massage or a special dinner out if you stick with your practice for a month. Whatever you do, keep trying. Find a balance between earnestly encouraging yourself and being gentle with yourself.

Meditation Techniques

Our Breath

Learning how to breathe deeply and properly can help us quickly shift out of a place of stress and into a place of calm focus. Therefore, learning breathing practices is where we will begin.

Our breath is both automatic and controllable. This is an important fact to consider when you also realize that your breath is intimately connected to your mental and emotional state. Think for a moment; if you're surprised, what happens with your breath? You sharply inhale or gasp a breath in. What does your breath do when you get disappointing news? You sigh as you exhale. What about when you're grieving? You gasp for breath amidst tears. And when you're under stress, you breathe very shallowly, perhaps only allowing the upper chest to move a little with each in and out breath.

It is important to understand this connection between breath and emotion and to remember that we have the wonderful ability to take control of our breath whenever we choose. It stands to reason, therefore, that by learning breathing patterns that calm us, help us focus, or sometimes even energize us, we can influence our experience in the moment. How powerful is that! Before we go further, here's an important disclaimer. I'm offering you breathing practices to help you step out of the rapids of a strong emotion so you might stand on the metaphorical riverbank and observe your emotion from a grounded place. That way, you can honor how you feel and feel it without drowning in it. That's different from using these practices to avoid your emotions. I don't recommend that, because as I've said before, there's no escape. If it's in us, we will eventually have to deal with it, and there's no time like the present moment. So please remember we are cultivating awareness, which means looking at everything in the dark recesses of our minds and hearts. It might not be easy at first, but these practices will hold your hand and help you see that you have the strength to be fully present in your life, no matter what's going on.

Diaphragmatic Breathing

Our bodies are designed to breathe using our diaphragms. The diaphragm is an umbrella-shaped sheet of muscle that's nestled up under the ribcage against the bottom of the lungs. When we inhale, it's because the diaphragm acts as a powerful suction, drawing air into the lungs as it flattens out downward into the abdomen. When the diaphragm draws down in this way, it literally pushes the abdominal organs a little forward, out of the way, so our belly expands or rises on the in-breath. When we exhale, it's because the diaphragm pushes upward again, up under the ribcage, pressing the air out of the lungs. Sometimes, you'll hear people refer to this as belly breathing. There is a whole host of benefits. Deep diaphragmatic breathing is calming to the nervous system, reduces heart rate and blood pressure, and can be refreshing mentally and emotionally. But why should we have to learn something that's natural? If you ever watch babies sleeping on their backs, you'll see this natural process. Their little chests don't move much at all, but you'll see their bellies rise as they inhale and fall as they exhale. The problem is that as we grow from infancy to adulthood, we accumulate stress. Remember how I mentioned the breath is tied to emotions? Well, the diaphragm and the lungs are physically affected by stress as well. When we are under stress, we can tighten up in the abdominal area. It's a protective reaction leftover from primitive times; we want to protect our chest and abdomen, where all our vital organs are. The problem is that this kind of deep tension can affect the muscle of the diaphragm itself and create dysfunctional patterns of breathing.

Untrained breathers often do what's called reverse breathing — inhaling into the chest while sucking the belly in, then exhaling as the belly distends. Reverse breathing actually restricts breathing and can increase feelings of anxiety because the diaphragm isn't working in the way it was designed. To combat this, we need to get the belly and diaphragm to relax. For most of us, the best way to do that is to lie down on your back. I recommend lying on the floor on some kind of mat or rug rather than a squishy bed surface; that way, your body is supported firmly and will not collapse in any way. You should not use a pillow under your head when doing this reclined breathing practice, either. If it is uncomfortable to lie with your head on the floor, fold a thin blanket several times and place it under your head or roll it and place it behind your neck. You want to maintain a straight spine so your breath can flow with the greatest amount of ease. Try to focus on these concepts of diaphragmatic breathing as you practice the following techniques.

3-Part Diaphragmatic Breathing

In the reclined position described above, place one hand on your belly and one hand on your upper chest. Before deepening your breath, observe your natural breath and which moves first, the belly or the chest. Notice where there is a fuller movement without changing anything. Then begin breathing deeply in these three parts:

1. Fill and expand the belly first.
2. Then, expand your ribcage.
3. Finally, lift the chest and collarbones at the upper limit of your inhale.

Then we exhale in reverse:

1. Upper chest relaxes.
2. Rib cage comes back to center.
3. Belly falls toward the spine.

So, 3-part breathing works like a wave: inhale belly, ribcage, chest…exhale chest, rib cage, belly.
Breathing in this way, you both allow your diaphragm to work as it was designed, as well as work the little muscles in between each of the expanded ribs. You are using your whole torso to breathe. As you begin a breath practice,

if you've never done anything like this before, it's normal to feel like you had a gentle workout to the ribs and abs because, in fact, you have. When doing a deep breathing practice, you want to try to make the breath as smooth and slow as possible. If you notice yours is choppy, don't worry. It will get smoother the more you practice.

The benefits of intentional deep breathing practices are numerous:

- They stimulate the vagus nerve, a major cranial nerve responsible for balancing the nervous system and lowering heart rate.

- They trigger the vagus nerve to release acetylcholine, a neurotransmitter that increases focus and calmness and decreases feelings of anxiety.

- When practiced consistently, deep breathing results in lower blood pressure and heart rate.

- When practiced in conjunction with mindfulness, it increases gray matter in certain regions of the brain.

With these benefits in mind, let's explore some more specific breathing techniques.

4:8 Breathing

This is my go-to stress-relieving practice and the favorite practice of thousands of people I've taught. It is simple and powerful, and it uses diaphragmatic breathing, which you've just learned.

1. Sit comfortably and either close your eyes or turn your gaze downward.
2. Take full, deep breaths.
3. Inhale and fill the lungs to a count of four.
4. Exhale and empty the lungs to a count of eight.
5. Repeat.
6. Try to just breathe through your nose. You may choose to exhale through your mouth if it's more comfortable.
7. Practice for between two and five minutes to start. Work your way up to ten minutes.

Variations:

- Elongate the breath: work toward eventually inhaling to 10, and exhaling to 20, but don't force or push yourself.
- Add the ocean breath sound: this is done by practicing with your mouth open first, making a "fog the mirror" sound as you exhale. Next, make the sound as you inhale also. Finally, try to make the sound with your mouth closed, just breathing through your nose. In the yoga tradition, they call this *ujjayi* breathing. It helps you focus, elongates the breath, and trains your relaxation response to kick in.
- Add a breath hold,

- only if you are free from the following conditions: pregnancy, uncontrolled high blood pressure, COPD, heart disease, glaucoma.

- The breath hold might be just a pause or the length of the inhale or exhale.

Start practicing 4:8 breathing on your own, both in moments of acute stress as well as regularly. I suggest practicing it as the same time each day, perhaps when you first wake up or when you get into bed at night. Notice a difference in how you feel. Ultimately, this practice will condition your parasympathetic nervous system (rest and digest) to be more active so you can feel calmer and more centered.

Square Breathing

This breath technique is used by Navy Seals to help them stay calm and focused. The pattern of counting, deep breathing, and breath-holding can help increase focused attention as well as cultivate a feeling of empowerment. As I mentioned previously, please be cautious with or avoid breath holds if you are pregnant, have COPD, anxiety, glaucoma, or uncontrolled high blood pressure. Otherwise, give it a try to see how it works for you.

1. Sit comfortably and either close your eyes or turn your gaze downward.
2. Begin to take deep breaths.
3. Inhale deeply to a count of 4.
4. Hold your breath for a count of 4.
5. Exhale fully to a count of 4.
6. Hold your breath out for a 4.
7. Repeat.

Variations:

- Elongate the length of your breath and the amount of time you hold, trying to keep an even pattern; for example, inhale to a count of 6, hold for 6, exhale for 6, hold for 6, repeat. Use whatever count feels best for you. Over time, you might feel like you can lengthen the time, but don't force or push yourself.

Notice how you feel when practicing 4:8 breathing as opposed to square breathing. Be patient with yourself. Sometimes, it takes quite a bit of practice to get comfortable with breathing techniques. Practice the one that resonates with you more, keeping the other in your metaphorical back pocket.

These next two breathing techniques are simple, in-the-moment practices to help you diffuse physical, mental, and emotional tension. They are not necessarily to be used as a seated practice you do for 10 minutes but rather when you notice stress arising in the body.

The Sigh

The "sigh" is a simple practice only requiring about one minute. Take a deep breath in, hold it for just one second, then exhale with an audible sigh. When I've taught this in classes, people sometimes seem self-conscious about making noise on their exhalation, but that's the best part. Exaggerate it, really let go, and "ahhh" out that exhale. Try to make noise last for the length of your long, slow exhale. It might feel dramatic or silly until you get used to it, but it is actually a fantastic, easy way to release stress and tension and turn your attention inward to observe sensations. Notice how you feel before the sigh and after you take between 3-5 sigh breaths.

Horse Lips

Horse lips breath is similar to the sigh because you are taking a deep breath in and pausing for a moment. But now, when you exhale, you're going to loosely keep your lips together as you blow air through them, making the sound you might hear a horse make. Once again, you might feel silly; however, this technique relaxes the muscles of the face and jaw, and the slow breaths, whatever the exhale sounds like, help to cue your nervous system to relax. Take at least three horse lips breaths whenever you notice tension in your face.

Mindfulness Meditation Techniques

Now that you've turned your attention inward and have learned to use breathing practices to shift out of a state of overwhelm, it is time to practice true mindfulness meditation. By that, I mean practices that encourage you to just be in the simplicity of the present moment, with awareness resting in whatever sensations, thoughts, or emotions rise and fall away. This kind of regular training enables you to live more mindfully by following the three A's of mindfulness and responding more skillfully to whatever life presents you. It won't be easy because the practice involves learning to sit with what may be uncomfortable. It forces you to face your internal demons, be they traumatic memories, mistakes you've made, losses you've endured, or grief you've suppressed. Practicing mindfulness meditation requires you to stop the glorification of being busy long enough to see clearly what you might be avoiding and to train yourself to accept — to be okay with — whatever state you are in. You need to see it, own it, feel it, and hold yourself with friendliness, compassion, and gentle care. If you can do that, sometimes you feel better without having to fix or change anything because you can make peace with the messiness of life. Intellectually, we all know that things change; life itself is impermanent. But we delude ourselves and distract ourselves away from this reality and into avoidance, where stress and resistance brew just beneath the surface until we are maxed out to the point where something must give. Sometimes, this is when people get sick with stress-related illnesses (hypertension, depression, anxiety, heart disease, cancer, auto-immune disorders, and more). Sometimes, this is when addiction begins, whether it is to drugs, alcohol, television, food, sex, or something else. Addiction often occurs as a simple desire to feel some sense of control when life feels out of control. Mindfulness practice is the ultimate practice of true self-control. You can learn to increase your tolerance for the uncomfortable, unpleasant parts of life and accept yourself just as you are in each moment, fully knowing that you are also capable of growth and improvement. This is how you take the reins of your life, manage stress, and feel better.

Before we move into mindfulness techniques, I'd like to share a story with you that I learned long ago, the origin of which I do not know.

A woman was having trouble sleeping. Her worst fears, in the form of three flying demons, swirled around her. These demons brought images of past trauma, of fears of the future, and whispered to her that all her insecurities were true. Finally, she just decided to get out of bed and go to the kitchen. The demons followed her. She put on a kettle of water and retrieved four teacups from the cabinet. When the demons realized that she was pouring four cups of tea and setting them at the table, they stopped transmitting their fear stories, and one of them said to her, "We are showing you your worst nightmares, trying to scare you. What are you doing?" She smiled and responded, "You've been here before, and you'll be here again. So, I figured, why not sit and have some tea?" It is said that when she accepted the presence of her internal demons, instead of resisting them, they slowly turned into a circle of friends.

In the story, accepting the demons doesn't mean believing them or their story. It doesn't mean she liked their presence or didn't want them to stop. But sometimes, the act of surrender, not in the sense of giving up, but in the sense of accepting reality in the moment, softens the internal battle to the point you realize it is you fighting with yourself. The moment you give up the fight, you feel peace. The formal practice of mindfulness might feel like fighting an internal battle because your inner demons will rear their ugly heads. Consider, with practice, that you might be able to just wave to them with a friendly hello and then let them go or let them be, instead of getting stuck in fear and avoidance. "Do not fear" appears hundreds of times in the Bible. It's a message that is also woven throughout many cultures and spiritual traditions. Perhaps it is a call for us to just be present and experience what life offers us, the pleasant and the unpleasant alike.

Try one of the following mindfulness practices for ten minutes a day for the next month (that can be two five-minute sessions or one ten-minute session). Notice if you're able to gaze fearlessly at what's inside of you and outside of you with awareness, curiosity, and patience.

Please note when doing all these practices that regardless of your meditation technique, it is important not to criticize yourself when your mind wanders. Don't buy into the story that "you can't" meditate because your mind is too busy. A busy mind is great! We aren't trying to completely empty your busy mind. If you have neural connections firing in your brain, you will have thoughts. And in fact, a busy mind gives us something to work with in meditation. Your job is to focus on the technique, and when your mind wanders, notice and say to yourself, *huh, my mind wandered; now I'm thinking about ice cream.* It doesn't matter if you've been thinking about ice cream for two minutes or ten minutes. The moment you realize that your mind has wandered is a moment of mindfulness. Let the thought go, then refocus on your technique. Sometimes, it helps to label the thought or distraction (clock ticking, thought about the past, thought about the future, my rambling inner narrator, my neighbor cutting grass, irritation arising in my body). Naming it helps you to place it aside and then refocus on your practice. This might happen a thousand times in a ten-minute sitting. That's okay! Try not to get frustrated, and if you do, notice and label the frustration. Connect with your patient inner observer. This is all part of your meditation practice. If your mind didn't wander, you couldn't do it. The technique is there to help you focus on the part of you that is like a flagpole, solid and anchored. Your wandering mind is the flag whipping in the wind. It's all about where you place your attention. Both are present. The more you begin to notice and feel the part of you that is anchored, the easier it will be to not be thrown off by the ramblings and worries of your mind.

Body Scan

A body scan is a mindfulness practice in which you systematically place your awareness on parts of the body, feeling sensation or lack thereof. It has been shown to

- Cultivate greater focus and attention.

- Promote relaxation in the body.

- Improve neural activity and increase gray matter in the prefrontal cortex, our executive functioning/impulse control center in the brain.

- Reduce activity and activation of the amygdala, the brain's stress center.

This is one of the primary techniques of mindfulness training. It is an important practice because as you get familiar with noticing and feeling the body in this focused way, your awareness and ability to sense the body will grow stronger. You might notice that particular areas of the body are chronically tense or constricted. You might find, as you work with the body, mind, and emotions, that they are connected. Bessel van der Kolk, a well-known psychiatrist, author, and researcher, has written a book called *The Body Keeps the Score*, in which he discusses his research on how trauma affects both the mind and body and often needs to be worked out through both, as opposed to just the mind. While some of this work encourages movement of the body, which we will get to in our Care section of this book, a body scan is a good place to begin the practice of turning inward to feel the parts of the body. While simple in theory, this technique can be challenging to practice on your own. It helps to be guided in it a few times, so you might want to access one of my online body scan recordings.[8]

There are multiple methods to scan the body; some start at the feet and work up the body toward the head, and others work from the head down. Simply place your attention on each body part without moving the part. You may or may not feel sensations in every area. It is okay if you don't feel the sensation. Your job is to silently say the part in your head and try to bring your attention to that part of the body. Try to focus on the present moment sensation and let go of any judging or story about a particular part. Even if you've experienced trauma in your body, with patience and a self-love focus, you can become comfortable doing a body scan. Then, you can do it either slowly or quickly, standing, sitting, or lying down. The following are instructions for a seated body scan.

1. Sit in a comfortable position and try to relax.

2. Take a deep inhale and exhale with a sigh. Close your eyes or gaze downward.

3. Focus your attention on the feet. Feel the soles of the feet, the toes,

the heel, the ankles, the calves, the backs of the knees, the back of the legs, the back of the hips, the lower back, the mid back, the upper back...

4. Bring your attention to the backs of the arms, the elbows, forearms, wrists, backs of the hands, the fingers, the palms, inner wrists, forearms, inner elbows, upper arms, tops of the shoulders...

5. Bring your attention to the back of the neck, back of the head, top of the head, forehead, right eyebrow, left eyebrow, space between the eyebrows...the eyes, the nose, the tip of the nose, right cheek, left cheek, mouth, jaw, chin, throat, the collarbones, center of the chest, abdomen, tops of the thighs, knees, shins, tops of the feet.

6. And now the whole right leg...the whole left leg...the whole right arm...the whole left arm...The front side of the body...the back side of the body...The whole head. The whole body together. The whole body together. The whole body together.

You can stay here, focusing your attention on the whole body. Or you can do the scan again. Sometimes, you might go through it slowly, sometimes rapidly. The more you get familiar with the practice and variations of the practice, the more you can guide yourself with more ease. This can be a helpful first step in mindfulness because you are focusing on something concrete in the present moment, and you're keeping your mind busy naming and feeling various body parts.

Internal Awareness

This is a practice of paying attention internally and can help you:

- Cultivate acceptance of present-moment circumstances as reality.

- Allow for greater focus, clarity, and decision-making.

- Develop awareness of the physical body, energy level, emotions, mood, and mental chatter to catch certain qualities when they are small and choose to take action to rebalance; for instance, noticing the emotion of frustration and choosing to do something to diffuse it before it grows into anger.

The practice of internal awareness can be done independently or to initiate another mindfulness technique. It is simple, but it can be challenging to practice because it involves taking an honest look at what's going on in the dark recesses of your body, your emotions, and your mind. Sometimes, this is not pleasant to do. Sometimes, we might want to judge ourselves for feeling a certain way, having a certain thought, or even for experiencing certain physical sensations.

Following these steps will help you notice what's happening inside and allow it to be there exactly as it is, without judgment. It's about learning to observe yourself from the outside, as a scientist would, by simply and dispassionately noting what is present.

1. Sit comfortably and either close your eyes or turn your gaze downward.

2. Bring your attention to your physical body. Notice physical sensations, particularly any that feel distracting, like tension in the shoulders or jaw, sensations of soreness or injury. Try not to be reactive to these sensations, but just observe them.

3. If possible, soften around the sensations, letting go of mental resistance to what is present.

4. Now, notice your energy level. In other words, are you tired, wide awake, or somewhere in between? Let go of judgment and story; just notice.

5. Notice your mood and emotions. Is there an underlying emotion present? Allow it to be there, and acknowledge it without judging yourself. Notice if there are sensations in the body that are connected to this emotion.

6. If possible, soften any resistance to this emotion.

7. Notice what's going on in your mind. Are your thoughts taking you to something that's already happened? To ideas or stories about the future? To your to-do list? Try to unhook yourself from being in the center of your thoughts and see if you can observe them, almost as if from the outside. Then, practice letting them float by.

Breath Awareness

In this practice, you are simply paying attention to your body's natural breathing process, focusing on sensations related to the breath. This practice:

- Cultivates focus and attention.

- Creates clarity and calms the mind with practice.

- Builds self-awareness, emotional regulation, and self-confidence.

- Builds patience and trust in self.

- Improves neural activity and increases gray matter in the prefrontal cortex, our executive functioning/impulse control center.

- Strengthens neural activity in the hippocampus and other memory and recall centers of the brain.

- Reduces activity and activation of the amygdala, the brain's stress center.

Breath awareness, called *anapanasati* in the Buddhist tradition, can be a very challenging practice because it is about letting go of control. Remember, the breath is a system that is both automatic and controllable. You can change your breath, breathe in certain patterns, hold your breath, and more. Because your brain knows this and likes order and control, it will attempt to control the natural breath. That is not the point of this practice. The point is to trust your body to breathe all on its own and simply bear witness to it. Feel the sensations associated with your breath. Your mind will wander, and it's your job to redirect it back to feeling sensations of the breath while letting go of the urge to change or control the breath, again and again.

1. Sit in a comfortable position and try to relax.

2. Choose a focal point for breath awareness. Either:

    a. Feel the flow of air in and out at the nostrils

    b. Feel the movement of your chest, ribcage, or belly

    c. Notice the sensations of breath somewhere else (wherever you feel it the most is where you should focus your attention).

3. Wherever you feel your breath the most is where you should focus your attention. That point is your anchor. Return your attention to feel the sensations of one breath at a time. One inhale and one exhale. And then another. Keep going.

4. If you find you're controlling your breathing, intentionally take a deep breath and begin again.

5. Practice for 3-5 minutes to start and work your way up to 10 minutes or more.

6. Be patient with yourself. Be gentle when calling your attention back.

Walking Meditation

Walking meditation is simple. Just slow down and be mindful of each step, wherever you are. It can be done anytime. For instance, you could park at the back of the lot when going to the grocery store or to work and practice walking meditation on your way to your destination. Or you could practice when going on a nightly walk around the neighborhood or hiking in the woods. It is a matter of coming home to your body and your breath again and again while moving through space. Most often walking meditation is practiced very slowly because we must slow down to pay attention. You can move at a micro-slow speed, or you can just slow down to half your normal pace. When practicing with a group, members might all walk together in a circle or in single file on a path. You could also walk slowly up and down the length of a yoga mat, almost like slow-motion pacing. I've even seen this practiced backward (for instance, take six slow steps forward, then six slow steps backward, and repeat).

The key is to keep your mind present with your body. If you are walking and thinking about your to-do list, it is not walking meditation. Feel free to walk with your hands on your belly, connecting with your breath, or clasp your hands lightly in front of you or behind you. Once again, this practice is different from how you might ordinarily walk. Slow down. Let go of the spiral of thoughts. Focus on your body moving through space or your feet on the ground. Return your attention to your body each time you notice you're thinking, each time you hear the rambling narrator inside your head. Give the narrator a nod, then turn away from it and focus on the sensation of walking. This is a great practice for people who struggle with sitting still. It's also a great way to start a longer meditation practice. Walk for several minutes, then settle into a seated position for practice. Doing this can help to quiet a noisy mind.

Gratitude & Positivity Practices

The mind is everything. What you think, you become. ~ the Buddha

Gratitude and positive psychology practices have gotten some attention in recent years because they can make you happier. There's also pushback against these practices. I've heard people call them toxic positivity, referring to the idea that positivity means we should ignore the tough things in life and only look at the rainbows and sunshine. This, however, is not what positive psychology practices are about.

Positive psychology is the scientific study of what makes life worth living and an applied approach to optimal functioning. It has also been defined as the study of the strengths and virtues that enable us, as both individuals and communities, to thrive. American psychologist Martin Seligman is considered the founding father of this movement, which began in the late 1990s. Positive psychology is a mindset that can be cultivated with mental exercise and practice to help shift one's perspective from flaws and scarcity to one based on strength and gratitude.

Creating a mindset of positive psychology can be challenging because, in our culture, we tend to operate on a deficit model:

- What is wrong?
- What did I do wrong?
- How can I avoid those errors in the future?
- What am I lacking?
- What do I wish I had?
- What are my flaws?

Whereas, in positive psychology, the questions are different:

- What is right and good in my life right now?

- What have I done well, with success, in the past?

- What enabled me to create that success?

- What are my strengths and best qualities?

- How can I utilize my strengths to work through challenges?

- What am I grateful for?

- How can I express that gratitude?

This is not to say that the first set of questions is wrong or bad or that we should never explore the answers to those questions. But we often don't get around to answering any questions like those posed in the second set, which are essential to our success and our sustained sense of happiness and well-being. I've included positive psychology practices in the section on mindfulness very deliberately. First, we must cultivate awareness of our current state; we must be able to look inside and see with clarity and acceptance what is rolling around in the depth of our minds, our psyche, our emotions, and even what is stuck energetically in our bodies. We must learn to sit with what's there, to welcome it, even, and to soften around the edges of the challenging parts. Then, we have an opportunity to take action in a positive way, cultivating gratitude and joy for ourselves. The fact of the matter is, that we all have difficult and unpleasant parts of our lives and beautiful parts of our lives for which we can be grateful. Positive psychology is about looking at both. We don't want to blind ourselves or turn away from the hard things but rather broaden our view to include the good things as well. Skillful living is being able to hold space for it all.

Don't feel bad if you're someone who tends to focus on the negative. Our brains are wired to do this as a defense mechanism. It goes back to that primitive wiring, looking for the angry bear who might be around any corner, waiting to attack you. However, we can train the brain to scan our environment for wonderful things and to retrain it to be more positive. This is a powerful ability because research shows that people who have more of a positive mindset are both more successful and happier![9]

Here are some practices to train the brain to see positive things:

- 30-day Gratitude Practice:

    o In the evening before bed, write in a journal 3-5 things you are thankful for that day. Do this exercise every day, and don't repeat anything. In other words, you can only be thankful for friends, family and pets one time. By eliminating repetitions, you'll be stretched to search for good things in your life, like running water and food to eat when you're hungry. Looking for the positive instead of falling into natural negativity will shift your perspective and rewire your brain.

- Random Acts of Kindness:

    o When in line at Starbucks, a highway toll plaza, or in other circumstances, anonymously pay for the person behind you. It might cost less than $5 but will benefit you with feelings of delight for doing something kind with no recognition.

    o Volunteer your time whenever possible, even if it's for one or two days every few months. You might serve food at a shelter, visit a nursing home, play with puppies at an animal shelter, or do something else for some population that is special to you. Selfless service benefits others, but the reward for us, mentally and emotionally, is double what we put out.

    o If you work in a city, notice people who look lost and offer to help them.

    o If you are out and about and notice anyone struggling, stop and offer to help them.

- Speak kindly to cashiers, baristas, servers, and other service people. Praise them for their work.

- Leave a note of thanks to your postal carrier, UPS driver, garbage collectors, or any other service individuals who come to your home.

- Smiles, Humor & Laughter:

    - Be mindful of your facial expressions. Try to smile more often. Make it a natural smile by thinking of something pleasant or something you're grateful for.

    - Have a handful of light, silly jokes you commit to memory. Pull one out when things are feeling heavy.

    - Try Laughter Yoga or Laughter Exercises. Simply get a group together and force laughter. Soon, everyone will be laughing at each other, pretending to laugh, and it will become natural.

- Create Your Own Counterfacts:

    - In every scenario, there are the facts of the circumstance and the hypothetical alternative circumstance or counterfacts that "might" have happened. In his book *The Happiness Advantage*, Shawn Achor provides this imaginary scenario for us to consider: You are part of a group of people in a bank when a robber comes in. You are the only one who gets shot when the robber fires his gun. You are shot in the arm. No one else is hurt. These are the facts. The question is, is this a fortunate circumstance or an unfortunate circumstance?[10] It depends on your perspective, which originates in your own hypothetical counterfacts. In this scenario, some might say it was unfortunate because they were the only one who was shot, while others might say it was fortunate because they were only shot in the arm, and no one else was hurt. The only difference is perspective, over which we have control. So why not train yourself to take the positive view as opposed to the negative? Achor calls this creating your own counterfacts.

Mindfulness: The Practice and the Life Skill

We are nearing the end of the section on mindfulness, but your work is just beginning. Try practicing each of the techniques I've offered, then take your favorite practices and create a daily routine for yourself. Ideally, you will practice for at least 10-15 minutes per day, even if it is two five-minute stretches. You're welcome to just use one technique for a while, then try another, or you can practice two back-to-back. For instance, I do 4:8 breathing for about 5-8 minutes a day; then I practice breath awareness for about the same amount of time in my daily 10-15 minute practice. It is recommended that you don't do a random practice every day because part of our intention is to cultivate focus and discipline. This comes when we only use one or two techniques regularly. If you wish to change techniques, do so monthly. Also, please try to practice on your own, as opposed to depending on recordings. Apps are great when you're learning, but one big goal of mindfulness is to cultivate self-awareness and self-control. This means we need to develop the skill of redirecting our own attention, again and again, without relying on anything external to our own being. I know it's challenging. I know your mind wanders. It will be okay. You will learn how to redirect your thoughts with practice and patience, I promise.

The mindset of mindfulness is one to adopt for life, so your practice doesn't end after your 15-minute timer rings. Mindfulness is not just a set of techniques, but its techniques are a kind of training or prep for application in the rest of your life. Notice opportunities to embody the three A's of mindfulness — they will arise any time you are frustrated, irritated, disappointed, or sad. Mindfulness doesn't offer a quick fix but rather a method of befriending yourself exactly as you are. It offers a place where you can hold your own hand and heart as you grow into your best self, one who is more focused, emotionally regulated, and resilient in the face of stress and challenge. Mindfulness requires practice and a growth-oriented mindset. It is necessary to be open and willing to soften, remove the armor of your ego, and consider broader perspectives. Some say it is a process of allowing yourself thousands of little deaths and births because we are always changing, and our circumstances are always changing. The intention of mindfulness is to notice all of it, make peace with all of it, and then practice moving forward with skillful action again and again. Punah punah.

As a way of holding yourself accountable, consider the suggested schedule at the end of the Care section to help keep you on track, as you integrate mindfulness and other practices into your life.

Part Two: Discovery
(Self-Study)

When you practice looking inward with mindfulness, it can be scary. As you metaphorically shine that bright flashlight of awareness around in the dark recesses of your mind, you might not like what you find. Discovery is a process of self-study, in which you get comfortable with yourself: your past, your mistakes, your triumphs, your gifts, your patterns, and your darkness. It's about understanding your motivations based on unconsciously programmed beliefs you might have and then considering if you want to choose something different that might better align with who you want to be. Finally, it's about realizing the struggle of the human condition — things we all suffer from — and how we can learn to shift our perspective and ride the waves of change.

Mindfulness practices are a necessary step on the path of discovery because to see yourself clearly, you must learn how to step outside of your mental and emotional pattern of self-enmeshment. We are all so entangled in our own thoughts and feelings that it may start to feel like that is all we are. In some ways, we are quite addicted to our emotions. Honestly, sometimes, we want to stay angry and hold resentment. We want to stay in a low mood because to pull ourselves out would take too much effort. Sometimes, we want to stay stuck in a belief system, most frequently the belief that tells us we're not good enough because it feels impossible to shift.

> *People have a hard time letting go of their suffering. Out of a fear of the unknown, they prefer suffering that is familiar.*
> *~ Thich Nhat Hanh* [11]

Because if you were to change, what would it be like? Fear is ready to sabotage you around every corner of growth, and it's something we will discuss in this section. The fact is, beliefs and thoughts are all just constructs in your mind that you can change with knowledge and intentional practice. (See the locus of control section below for more on this). Yes, you can reprogram yourself. You can make what you want of this life. You don't have to feel at the mercy of your circumstances or whatever fleeting emotion is drowning you in the moment. To be in a state of self-knowing, self-understanding, and discovery is to learn what empowerment is. Perhaps you believe things happen for a reason, or you're willing to believe that we can create meaning in our lives. I believe that finding the space to understand ourselves and the universe enables us to choose what we want to do with this life. You can stay as you are and admire the philosophy of everything discussed in these pages, or you can decide to transform by doing the hard work necessary to cultivate the discipline to live skillfully on a path of purpose.

As we proceed, you'll be asked to either journal or ponder questions like: Who am I? What are my strengths? What are my patterns? What do I need? What do I want? What do I *really* want? These exercises will come after a reading or a prompt to get you stepping outside of your usual ways of thinking. Don't worry, I won't just randomly ask questions and then expect you to discover yourself and be transformed. I am here to guide you.

Let's begin with a model from ancient yoga philosophy called the *koshas*.

The Koshas

The koshas were first discussed in an ancient Vedic text called Taittiriya Upanishad, around the Sixth Century B.C. as a system of connecting mind, body, and spirit for the purposes of self-realization and spiritual connection.

The system of the koshas reminds us that we are complex, multi-dimensional beings made up of five layers or sheaths that together compose a human life. It is helpful to take ourselves apart in this way so that when we piece ourselves back together, we have a deeper understanding of which layer is being impacted by the events of our lives. Looking at ourselves like this can help us untangle our internal reactions to what we are experiencing and see another perspective with greater clarity.

When I'm teaching the koshas to a group, I ask for six volunteers to help me demonstrate. I arrange them in a single file line so that if you look at the line head-on, you only see one person.

Each person represents a layer of an individual being. The first five are the kosha layers, which we will go over, and the sixth represents the soul (or your best self, depending on your view). As I'm introducing each, I'll lead with the traditional Sanskrit name, but for ease of understanding, I'll primarily refer to their English translations. The kosha layers are all part of us, and we are entangled with them. However, all we see in each other, and sometimes in ourselves, is the first layer.

Annamaya Kosha (Physical Layer)

This is, most obviously, our physical body. It is what we see in the mirror, what we can touch, what others see and can touch. This is the part of us that can get out of balance when we are sick, injured, or in pain. When something is amiss in the physical body, it's hard to focus on any other dimension of being. What we can do is recognize that the physical body is part of but not all of who we are. Mindfulness helps us notice and experience what's going on in the body. We can begin by seeing the cause and effect that different foods, activities, and mental states have on our physical bodies. Then, we can then care for our physical body by eating healthy food, staying hydrated, exercising, resting, and doing physical practices that help to release tension and cultivate ease. It is important to remember that this outer layer is all we see of each other. The other layers are deep within.

Pranamaya Kosha (Energy Layer)

Behind the physical layer is our energy. This "life force" layer is connected to our vitality and our breath. When you're tired, when you're stressed, or when you're feeling depleted, this layer is negatively impacted. It's also positively impacted when you feel connected to people, circumstances, and places. When this layer is balanced, not only do we feel well-rested but we also have a zest for life. This is why it's important to get a good night's sleep each night and to engage in activities you feel passionately about. Breathing exercises are also vital to help manage this layer. It's important to be aware of this layer and be curious about any imbalances you detect.

Manomaya Kosha (Mental & Emotional Layer)

Behind our body and our energy is our mental-emotional self. This third layer overtakes and influences the physical and energy layers again and again. We live much of our lives inside our own minds and the emotions that result from the story we cling to. Mark Twain humorously referred to this state of mind by saying, "I've lived through some terrible things in my life, some of which actually happened."

How much do we suffer, not because of our circumstances, but because of a story we repeat in our minds, again and again? We are mentally and emotionally affected by all the "what ifs" and "if onlys", by our fears lived out as conversations in our heads and by imagined responses from others that fuel our sadness, our anger, and our frustration. I once heard meditation teacher Jack Kornfield share a Buddhist teaching from the Sallatha Sutta on suffering in a parable about two arrows. When something hurts us, we are pierced with two metaphorical arrows. The first, which we have no control over, is the moment an unpleasant event happens; it feels like we are hit with an arrow, and it causes pain. The second is the one with which we stab ourselves with again and again every time we relive the event in our minds. We can choose to set aside this second, self-inflicted arrow, so we do not cause ourselves repeated pain. It is important to get to know this layer of your being. Discover how you are internally stabbing yourself inside and consider what it would take to stop this behavior and balance this part of yourself. Mindfulness, breath work, therapy, talking with friends, and spiritual practice can all be tools to help you understand when you are stuck in this layer and determine how to recenter again and again.

Vijnanamaya Kosha (Wisdom Layer)

This fourth layer, hidden behind the first three, is often called the layer of discernment or deep wisdom. This is not intellect in terms of the thinking mind but rather an embodiment of intuition and inner knowing beneath the noise of the mind. This layer is underdeveloped in people who struggle to make up their minds or who have poor judgment and lack the application of personal ethics. Spiritual practice and meditation will help strengthen this kosha layer. It is a vital part of being that all humans possess. It can easily be blocked by an imbalance in the first three kosha layers. More on this later.

Anandamaya Kosha (Bliss Layer)

The fifth kosha is the innate capacity for joy that is within all of us. Think of a time when you felt a sense of deep inner happiness that wasn't necessarily related to circumstances. Can you remember a moment when you felt such positive inner excitement you could just explode? The bliss layer is the exuberance, vitality, and childlike wonder that we can access throughout our lifespan when we work through our imbalances in our first three layers of the koshas.

How You Can Work with the Koshas

Behind the five layers of the koshas is our higher self, which you may think of as your soul or just the very best version of yourself. Ideally, our higher self will shine through all the layers of the koshas so we have a healthy physical body, feel a high level of energy, learn the resilience necessary for mental-emotional balance, access the deep wisdom needed to respond skillfully in life and experience joyful bliss.

However, this doesn't always happen because as humans, we experience challenge, difficulty, and trauma. Our first three kosha layers, the physical, the energy, and the mental-emotional, can be significantly impacted by what happens in our life circumstances. They get bound up, unbalanced, blocked. We have physical pain, we are exhausted, and we experience varying levels of anxiety or depression. When the first three koshas are in this state, we have limited access to our wisdom, innate bliss, or our higher self. Ultimately, we can't deepen our experience of life unless we learn what is going on with our first three koshas and what we can do to cultivate an ongoing state of equilibrium in each of them. This won't be a one-and-done process but rather a lifelong course of checking in with awareness and compassion. You can't push away or deny imbalance. You have to face it head-on and learn to move through it or rise above it. The first step is getting curious about what's going on inside you, as opposed to being afraid to see it. And there's no time like the present to start.

So right now, take a few slow, deep breaths and relax. Breathe in, breathe out. Feel the connection you have to the ground; perhaps that's feet on the floor, or perhaps your body is lying in bed, and you can connect to that plane of support. Just for a moment, feel it, the support from underneath you. Inhale, exhale. Ask yourself the following questions and either journal your answer, allowing yourself the space to write as much or as little as you'd like, or just close your eyes and ponder the questions, one by one.

Focus on your physical body:

- What's going on in your body these days?
- When did any discomfort/illness/imbalance begin?
- What else was happening at that time?
- How do you manage pain in your body?
- Have you ever considered that your mental/emotional state impacts your physical body? How so?
- What do you do to care for your physical body?
- What could you do more of or less of?

Focus on your level of energy or vitality:

- Do you feel well-rested most days of the week?
- Do you have good "sleep hygiene?" (More on this in the Care part of the book)
- Are you dependent on caffeine or medication to wake you up in the morning?
- When was the last time you felt full of vigor and excitement? What was going on?
- What are you passionate about?
- Do you feel that you tend to have high energy or low energy?
- How often do you think about or do something to influence your energy?
- Do you practice breathing techniques daily? Are you willing to start?

Focus on your mental-emotional state:

- Do you worry that things won't go as you planned in the future?

- Do you frequently lament the past?

- Are you able to focus your attention for as long as you'd like?

- Do you often feel like a bear is attacking you, even when small things don't go your way?

- How do you handle stress? Do you feel it is working for you?

- What's your biggest fear right now?

Explore and consider your answers, and if you don't have answers, practice some mindfulness techniques and ask yourself again in a week or so. There are no answers or ways to assess where you are on some contrived scale. These questions are designed to help you explore yourself and your inner world. The more you can be curious and honest with yourself as you delve into the first three koshas, the sooner you'll be able to tap into the last two koshas, wisdom, and bliss, where you will access intuition and deep joy.

Wisdom questions:

- What is your deepest longing in life?

- What is the biggest question you have for yourself?

- Close your eyes. Take five slow breaths. Then ask yourself:

- What's the answer to your question? Listen to the first response from inside. Is it your sarcastic mind, or is it from a deep inner place? Do you know for certain? Keep asking and keep listening.

Bliss questions:

- When was the last time you had a big, full-belly laugh?
- Who were you with?
- When's the last time you felt like smiling because you felt a deep inner joy?
- What were you doing, and where were you?

I've intentionally started the discovery section with the koshas because many concepts I'll be discussing relate to exploring the koshas, especially that pesky mental-emotional one. Our thoughts and emotions tend to run our lives. By cultivating a greater understanding of our beliefs, our autopilot way of thinking, and our emotional reactions, we can make space for shifts in perspective, processing, and, in our actions moving forward.

Locus of Control

Do you believe you are a creator of your life's circumstances? Or do you believe that things are mostly outside of your control? Psychologist Julian B. Rotter came up with the concept of locus of control in 1954, and it continues to play an important role in personality studies and psychology today.

Locus of control is the idea that we have an internal or external locus of control. If you have an external locus of control, you believe that your life circumstances happen entirely by chance and other people's influences; you have little control. With an internal locus of control, you think your actions matter, and you can create your path in life. Many people are not entirely one way or the other; rather, locus of control can fall on a spectrum.

So, what's your locus of control? Which of the following sets of questions sounds more like you?

Outlook 1

- Bad things happen in life due to bad luck.

- It doesn't matter how hard I work; it won't make a difference in the long run.

- People don't get what they deserve; it's all just random.

Outlook 2

- If I work hard, I can achieve anything I put my mind to.

- Luck has nothing to do with success; it's all hard work, determination, and a positive attitude.

- Disappointments often happen because of mistakes I've made.

If the statements of Outlook 1 resonate more, you likely have an external locus of control. If Outlook 2 makes sense to you, you have an internal locus of control. Or perhaps you're somewhere in between, depending on the circumstances. Although some believe that your locus of control is set in childhood, others believe you can shift it. This is important because there is a correlation between a strong internal locus of control, self-efficacy, and resilience. In other words, the more you feel you have control over your well-being, circumstances, and life at large, the greater your ability to cope with stress and be motivated to make necessary changes in your life. Studies also show that with an internal locus of control, you're ultimately more successful in both work and your personal life.[12]

With a greater external locus, you believe things are outside of your control, sometimes to the point of helplessness. This kind of mindset can make you feel like a constant victim, powerless to change. It can lead one toward depression or living in a general state of unhappiness.

So, what can you do if you fall on the external locus spectrum?

To shift more toward an internal locus of control, start to notice how you initially view circumstances and events. Do you feel like a victim, or can you take action or responsibility? Consider viewing yourself as a more active participant in your life, as opposed to a bystander. Take action where you ordinarily would not, simply as an experiment to see if it changes an outcome. Start small, either by considering a shift in attitude, even if you have to fake it, or doing something you wouldn't ordinarily do. Little by little, you can prove that your actions do matter. If you're reading this book, I have to believe that you are at least on a path toward an internal locus of control, so that's great! Keep going. We all can learn to shift toward feeling more empowered and in control of what happens to us and how we respond to it.

Strengths-Based Mindset

To help strengthen the view that you can be a creator of your life's path, it is vital to know what you are already doing well. As I mentioned in the gratitude and positivity practices section, sometimes modern thinking pushes us toward a deficit model: we ask ourselves, *how will I screw up this time?* Or we think of what we lack. What if we instead asked ourselves, *what is good in my life right now?* Or if we think of our strengths? What's that, you ask? Are there crickets chirping in your head as you consider what you're good at? No, I'm not talking about your ability to sing, knit, or rebuild an engine. Strengths aren't silly human tricks or abilities, either. I'm talking about personality strengths.

Personality strengths are what naturally help you get through challenging times, and they're often part of the reason why other people like you. We all have character strengths, though they might be wildly different from each other. It's challenging to recognize what we do naturally, so it might be helpful to start by asking your best friend what he or she likes about you or what she thinks your strengths are. Can you imagine what your friends might say about you? Take a moment to close your eyes and think about this or journal about it.

It's also sometimes helpful to take a quiz to uncover your strengths. The VIA character strengths survey is a great validated tool used by positive psychologists, and you can take it online for free at www.viacharacter.org. They'll give you your top five strengths, drawing from qualities like bravery, creativity, curiosity, forgiveness, gratitude, honesty, hope, humor, wisdom, kindness, leadership, love, perseverance, perspective, self-regulation, spirituality, and more. When you take the test, answer the questions as quickly as possible with your initial instinct. Don't overthink the questions. Once you get your results, reflect on your top strengths, recalling specific instances when you've called on these qualities to get you through difficult times. Journal about it if writing is helpful for you.

Keep a card in your wallet or a photo on your phone with a list of your top five strengths. Look at it occasionally to remind yourself what you have on your side. Anytime you are down and struggling, look at that list of five strengths and ask yourself first if you're utilizing these strengths, and if not, how you might call them forward to give you another perspective or even help to solve an issue.

During a time when I was at a really low point, struggling with grief and big changes in my life, I recalled my five strengths from the VIA. I particularly remembered that my top strength was spirituality. I realized that I was suffering so much because I wasn't looking at things through the lens of this strength. I had allowed it to fall away. That became a lightbulb moment for me to renew my habits and practices that helped cultivate that quality, and I was able to heal and move forward in life. Your strengths can do the same for you.

Intelligence

In addition to personality strengths, we all have different kinds of intelligence. Again, this is not necessarily about being able to do advanced mathematics, translate scientific equations, or write an award-winning poem. Rather, intelligence can be about how we process information and use it to take action.

Emotional Intelligence

It's become a catchy concept these days: EQ, as opposed to IQ (emotional quotient to intelligence quotient). Emotional intelligence refers to a person's self-awareness, self-control, social skills, empathy, motivation, and decision-making skills. Do these qualities sound familiar in regard to concepts we've already discussed? I hope so because mindfulness skills are a big part of increasing emotional intelligence.

Self-awareness is your ability to look inside and recognize when you are stuck in your perspective or in a grumpy mood. It's all about noticing what's going on inside, just like the practice of mindful internal awareness. Self-regulation or self-control is choosing how you take action when you notice yourself out of balance. It's being able to answer the question, *what is a healthy way for me to cope with my angsty feelings?* Then it's about following through with that action to maintain self-control, instead of having a knee-jerk emotional reaction. In our Connection part of the book, we will discuss the emotional intelligence quality of having effective social skills, which involve forming and maintaining relationships utilizing positive communication skills.

Perhaps the most critical emotional intelligence quality is empathy, or the ability to deeply understand how others are feeling and respond skillfully and with compassion. Finally, motivation and the ability to make quality decisions are included in the discussion of emotional intelligence because they refer to individuals' drive to improve themselves for their internal satisfaction and growth. Emotional intelligence also considers one's ability to move forward by choosing the best option based on one's values and morals.

Where are you on the emotional intelligence scale, and how can you improve? There are plenty of online quizzes to help assess your EQ. Still, I think it is also something you can reflect and journal about by honestly exploring each of these qualities and considering where you have the strength and where you could grow: self-awareness, self-control, social skills, empathy, motivation, and quality decision-making skills. Remember not to criticize yourself for any perceived deficit you have. The purpose is to stay open-minded and open-hearted and be curious about yourself. We all have strengths and growth edges. Your job is to celebrate your strengths and see if you can shift positively in a new direction where you haven't before, little by little. Punah punah.

Myers-Briggs Personality Typing

You might have heard of Myers-Briggs Personality Typing, which was developed by Isabel Briggs Myers and her mother, Katherine Briggs, in the 1960s. It is based on the work of the psychologist Carl Jung and involves typing people on a spectrum of four categories:

- Introversion vs. Extraversion
- Sensing vs. Intuition
- Thinking vs. Feeling
- Judging vs. Perceiving

Each category refers to a preference or style of being that individuals tend toward. Where they fall on each of these creates a set of four letters: ENFJ, for instance, refers to someone who is more extroverted, intuitive, feeling, and judging. Let's explore the meanings of each.

Introversion vs. Extraversion (I or E):
What recharges you? Introverted individuals tend to be energized by spending time alone or perhaps with a select few others. Introverts can be more reserved in their behavior and are more thoughtful. Extraverts are energized by spending

time with people and often thrive in busy, fast-paced surroundings. They can be very expressive and outspoken. You might be at one end of the spectrum, or you could be very much in the middle if you experience both at times.

Sensing vs. Intuition (S or N):
How do you process information? Those who are Sensing focus on their five senses; they connect more with information they can see, hear, and feel. They are tactile or hands-on learners and might be considered more practical. Intuitives focus on instinct or intuition; they are more interested in theories and patterns and are often regarded as creative.

Thinking vs. Feeling (T or F):
How do you make decisions? With your mind or with your heart? Thinkers are more rational and logical. Feelers are interested in how something affects people and whether it aligns with their values.

Judging vs. Perceiving (J or P):
How do you approach structure in your life? Those who fall in the Judging category appreciate structure. They like things planned and dislike last-minute changes. Perceivers tend to be flexible and spontaneous. They want to be free to change their minds.

Have you taken a Myers-Briggs quiz before, or can you guess where you'd fall in each category? Keep in mind that they fall on a spectrum. For instance, I technically classify as an extrovert, but when I took the test, it showed I was just over the border from introvert to extrovert, which is important because sometimes I have those introvert tendencies, too. The official Myers-Briggs test requires a fee, but there are some knock-off quizzes online that are fairly accurate. Consider learning about yourself through this lens of personality to better understand your motivations and reactions to what happens to you in life, what you need, and how you can utilize the forms of intelligence you already possess.

Enneagram Personalities: Head, Heart, or Gut Intelligence

While the origin of the Enneagram Personality Typing isn't known, it is believed to have roots in ancient Greek philosophy, Jewish Kabbalah, Christian Mysticism, and even Sufism. The Enneagram has been used since the 1960s for personal self-knowledge and development. To summarize the complex personality system, there are nine types categorized under three centers of intelligence: head types — those who are more intellectual and thinking oriented, heart types — those who react more with emotions and emotional intelligence; and gut types — those who connect with their body's instinct and inner knowing. Each type within those three categories has its own motivations, fears, and internal dynamics and explores how they are related to other types on the scale. The nine personality types are:

- Heart:
    - Type Two, The Giver
    - Type Three, The Achiever
    - Type Four, The Individualist
- Head:
    - Type Five, The Investigator
    - Type Six, The Skeptic
    - Type Seven, The Enthusiast
- Gut:
    - Type Eight, The Challenger
    - Type Nine, The Peacemaker

o   Type One, The Reformer

If you've not heard of the Enneagram, I highly recommend looking up a quiz online and finding out where you fall. There are books, courses, and even practitioners who teach and counsel using the Enneagram due to the layers of connection and complexity of the types and their interdynamics with other types. It's much more than I can cover in these pages. When you find your type, you can gain quite a bit of insight into cycles you've experienced in your life and your auto-pilot reactions. Then, you can grow from this knowledge. I believe the Enneagram is an accurate personality typing system that explains our intelligence and strengths. It also addresses fears, which is something that is sometimes lacking in other assessments.

Fear

This brings us to our next section in Discovery: learning about your dark side. It is essential to see and accept all aspects of who you are, including what's in the dark recesses. Some refer to this as "shadow work." In an effort to learn more about fears that may be holding you back, you need to look within and ask yourself some really challenging questions.

Sometimes, we aren't aware of what frightens us because we are so tangled up in emotional reactivity. Emotions like frustration, irritation, offense, anger, resentment, sadness, and grief are all manifestations of fear at their core, and they mask the fear that's underneath. Because we feel these unpleasant feelings so deeply, they can become all-consuming. The mind then reinforces the emotion with a justified story to keep the fear present and growing like a fast-spreading virus. When we are stuck in a state of fear, our brain's primitive amygdala takes over and triggers the nervous system into feeling that this is a life-or-death circumstance even when it's not.

Think about a time when you got really frustrated or even angry. How long did it take to let go and move past it? Or is some part of you still angry after a significant amount of time? It takes a tremendous amount of patience, practice, and perseverance to learn how to step outside of fear and take a cold, hard look at what's really going on. Sometimes, we've buried our feelings or the experience of a traumatic event so deeply within that we don't know why we are stuck, sad, or angry. Often, we aren't afraid of what we think we are. Exploring common themes with which all human beings struggle can help us understand the nature of our own fear.

Attachment and Aversion

There is a classic Buddhist teaching about hope and fear, otherwise known as attachment and aversion, called the Eight Worldly Dharmas (or concerns). These concerns are described in four opposite pairs:

- Hope for happiness and fear of suffering (pleasure and pain)

- Hope for fame and fear of insignificance (fame and disrepute)

- Hope for praise and fear of blame (praise and blame)

- Hope for gain and fear of loss (success and failure)

You might read these and say, "Well, of course, I hope for those things, and I don't want the opposite. Who would?"

It's human nature to cling to what is pleasant and to have an aversion to what is unpleasant. Most of the choices we make involve avoiding what is unpleasant and acquiring more of what makes us feel good. Modern-day marketing depends on this: "Our product can make your life easier; you can't live without it." Start to pay attention to advertising that both obviously and subtly preys on fear, fear that we aren't enough, we don't have enough, we can't do enough, and we won't be happy unless (some caveat). Absolutely every product beyond those that meet our basic needs is triggering our desire to experience comfort instead of discomfort. There's nothing necessarily wrong with seeking comfort, but we must remain aware that throughout life, we will experience the full range of hopes and fears: pleasure and pain, fame and disrepute, praise and blame, success and failure. There is no way to buy or avoid our way out of this fact.

Looking deeper, we know that some of the circumstances that happen to us in life, the losses, the failures, the mistakes, and the betrayals, will sometimes feel unbearable. We will experience pain and dissonance for which no solution exists. We will have dark days because it's part of the human experience. That darkness and the suffering will vary greatly from person to person.

In the book *Man's Search For Meaning*, Viktor Frankl, discusses the psychology of what happens to human beings in such dire and abusive circumstances. When contemplating his experience in a Nazi prison camp, he comments, "If there is a meaning in life at all, then there must be a meaning in suffering."[13] Meaning in our suffering? How can we find meaning in pain? I mentioned the concept of post-traumatic growth in the introduction, the idea that from challenging circumstances, we can arise with greater wisdom and a renewed appreciation for life. But how can this happen if growing from adversity doesn't come naturally to you? When you're feeling mental, emotional, and even physical anguish, it might feel like you can't shift out of that pain to see anything else.

Mindfulness can offer us a gift in this regard. It can help us back out of the fear and suffering cycle and lessen our experience of our pain. How? Because pain starts with a root sensation, let's use physical pain as an example of the fear and suffering cycle. Imagine you've injured your lower back. The physiological sensation is obvious, but we unintentionally and unconsciously add multiple layers of suffering. Here are some ways we increase our experience of pain:

- Resistance: We first have resistance to the pain because who would want pain? We don't want it to be there, so we tighten up around the idea of its presence mentally, emotionally, and physically. We get angry or sad that we have pain. This is resisting the reality that the pain is there. And this resistance creates a layer of suffering.

- Past: Next, we might remember a similar kind of pain we experienced in the past, and we wonder if this pain will be as bad as that or worse than that. In essence, we are bringing our pain from the past into the present, so our experience of the present moment pain increases.

- Future: Then we might worry about when and if the pain will go away in the future. We are anticipating future pain, and unfortunately, that means we are suffering more in the present.

- Personal Fear and Identification: We have other personal fears around pain. Perhaps we've heard stories about this kind of pain and how bad it can get, and those thoughts are with us constantly, increasing our level of suffering. And finally, we might identify with the pain so much that we forget that we are much more than our pain. It becomes who we are and how we identify ourselves.

All these layers are fear-based and prey on us, triggering the mind-body pain connection (see next section) and increasing our experience of the pain we feel.

Fear is part of the human experience, but we don't have to be controlled by it. In the words of the Buddha, "Praise and blame, gain and loss, pleasure and sorrow come and go like the wind. To be happy, rest like a giant tree in the midst of them all." This goes back to the three A's of mindfulness: awareness, acceptance, and (skilled) action. Acceptance, perhaps, is the most important quality because it can calm the fear response with practice. Fear is part of the human experience, but we don't have to be controlled by it. The next several sections will help you discover your fear triggers, provide some tips and tricks on how to minimize them, and explain why this is so important for your mental, emotional, and physical well-being.

But before you move forward, look again at the eight worldly concerns and consider where your fear triggers might fall within these: fear of pain, disrepute, blame, or failure. What are you most afraid of? When have you experienced this in your life? How did you respond? Remember to be honest with yourself and don't judge yourself for your fear. What layers of suffering did you add on to the experience (resistance, past, future, personal fear)? Are you willing to try to let some of this go since it is a construct your mind has created?

Pondering these questions is an exploratory exercise designed to help you understand yourself in a deeper way, so look with curiosity. In my opinion, the "why" of the fear is less important than just having an awareness of it and noticing your patterned response to it. We often can't change the why as it likely has to do with past circumstances. But we can learn to see our fear and respond to it differently by cutting through the layers of suffering, learning to breathe, softening our emotions, and accepting the present moment for what it is, even when we don't like it. We do have this choice.

Frankl reminds us that "everything can be taken from a man but one thing: the last of the human freedoms—to choose one's attitude in any given set of circumstances, to choose one's own way."[14] He says this when describing various men's reactions to being in the concentration camps, where they were starved, beaten, and forced to work in the cold with little more than a thin layer of clothing. And yet he also observed men helping each other, finding moments of humor and even appreciating the beauty of a sunrise as they marched to dig ditches or to their deaths. Some men behaved reprehensibly as well, but the point is that there is a choice. If human beings in such dire circumstances as a concentration camp can choose a positive attitude and positive behavior, surely, we can step outside our privileged (in comparison) life and shift our attitude even regarding our pain and suffering. It's not an easy choice or an easy shift, but perhaps if we look at our lives as limited and finite, it might be easier to let go of our preferences and seek what we can appreciate in any given moment. Perhaps we can make a choice that we can feel good about instead of being dragged deeper into misery by our autopilot.

For most of us who aren't in such distressing situations, the easiest way to approach attachment (what you want) and aversion (what you fear) is to start small. What annoys you? How come? What's the real underlying reason for the irritation? Most often, if we are honest with ourselves, we might find that much of what we fear or have an aversion to has to do with a deep desire for control over our circumstances. We simply want things the way we want them (attachment). It's interesting because we tell young children having temper tantrums that they can't always get their way. Yet here we are in adulthood, wanting things to always be our way, exactly as we envision them. Whether it's fear of the unknown, uncertainty, or a lack of control, we have a strong dislike or an aversion to change. We are mentally attached to the positive ideas in our minds or positive circumstances when they occur. We want those pleasant moments to happen continually and last forever.

To soften your attachment and aversion, let's start small by imagining something you can look at as an annoyance and simply accept it as it is. What if you could simply drop an attitude of dislike by practicing being an observer instead of being so enmeshed in your preference? As the observer, you look inside your own mind and say, *wow, look at how I dislike that. Isn't that interesting?* You're not forcing a thought or forcing positivity; you're simply practicing disidentification with the part of you that is irritated. You are not the irritation. You are not the fear. You are the one who can step back and watch it all. The interesting thing is that once you connect with this part of yourself, the part that is neutral and curious about life, the more in control you feel.

You will find that you are in control of yourself. Little by little, by practicing acceptance of things that differ from what you prefer, you will learn how to soften and embody the quality of equanimity: knowing you are and feeling okay, feeling peaceful, regardless of your circumstances. Thich Nhat Hanh shares his thoughts on acceptance in his book *No Mud, No Lotus: The Art of Transforming Suffering*, "Without mud, there is no lotus."[15] To me, he is saying that beauty often arises from imperfect circumstances. When we learn to compost our irritations, our challenges, and our traumas and allow them to nourish us and our perspective, we might grow stronger, brighter, and more compassionate. As we grow, our perspectives and purposes become clearer, making it easier to take skilled action.

Mind-Body Connection

Realizing that our minds and bodies are connected is not difficult. When you're stressed or nervous, does your stomach ever feel uncomfortable? Have you felt tension in your shoulders or jaw when you're under pressure? When you get a massage, how do things shift for you mentally and emotionally? Start to be mindful of how your body feels when you're in different mental and emotional states:

- How does your body feel when you are laughing?

- How does your body feel when you are rushed and stressed?

- How does your body feel when you're arguing with someone or when you get disappointing news?

There's a major cranial nerve called the vagus nerve. This "wandering nerve," which is the longest of its kind, is responsible for various internal functions of the body: respiration, digestion, heart rate, and some reflex actions like coughing and sneezing. A major regulator of the parasympathetic nervous system, this nerve links your brain to the neurons in your gut (the enteric nervous system) in a bi-directional way. This gut-brain connection explains why disorders of the gut, like IBS, are often associated with anxiety. And sometimes, a poor diet that disrupts the microbiome of the gut can *cause* anxiety. A growing body of research discusses the connection between stress, inflammation, and mood. This is important information because it is further evidence that you need to have a broader perspective if you want to live your best life. This isn't just about mental exercise; it's about a whole mind, emotion, and body experience. A great book about the gut-brain connection is called *The Second Brain* by Michael D. Gershon.

I invite you to explore how your body responds to the circumstances in which you find yourself. You might notice that your body shares its wisdom before your mind or emotions. The next time you watch a scary movie, take note of what happens in your body. How do you feel physically? What about when you get bad news? Where do you feel it in your body? How about if you are meeting someone for the first time? Do you ever get a "gut" feeling about them, whether you like them or not? Do you get a feeling in your stomach? Your shoulders? Your head (as in a headache)?

Getting familiar with your body's response to life is part of knowing yourself more deeply. This kind of deep self-knowledge offers a different understanding of the world around you. The more you practice, the more in tune you'll feel, and eventually, the more effortless recognizing the mind-body connection will become. Incorporating your new mind-body wisdom into your everyday awareness will help you move forward with greater clarity and less of a physical stress reaction.

Being Uncomfortable

When we start to step outside of our comfort zone, that's when the fear response kicks in, and our sympathetic nervous system can start to take over. The trick here is to notice when this begins to happen. If we can catch it at the start, it's a lot easier to connect with awareness and simply say to yourself, *Oh! Here's that fear response!* Then you don't have to respond. You can just watch it, sit with it, and feel it as a curious observer.

This awareness is challenging to practice in big, life-altering situations, so start small. What makes you irritated or uncomfortable? Long lines? Certain sounds? A talkative stranger? Notice your irritation as it arises and realize that it is inside of you. It's not coming from the outside, whether you choose to admit it or not. It is how your autopilot responds to that stimulus. Just because that's an auto-response doesn't mean you are at its mercy. You will find, if you are willing to practice, that you can change your internal and your external reactions to stimuli. This is one of the most empowering facts we can realize as human beings. It all starts with getting used to being uncomfortable.

I was lucky to realize this when I was in my 20s. I worked in marketing and public relations for a company in downtown Pittsburgh. I lived in a northern suburb and had a congested 30+ minute commute each way. People who know me now laugh when I tell this story because the truth is that I had road rage. When I fought traffic, I felt like one of those cartoon characters with red faces and steam shooting out their ears with a loud whistle. I'd swear and sometimes scream. More than that, I felt terrible inside. The level of stress was like lava in my veins, and it was more than I could bear. I hated driving. It wasn't until after my first yoga class that I gained enough self-awareness to realize that it was me. It was me who was freaking out about driving. The traffic simply was reality, a reality that was outside my control. And it scared me to realize that so much of the reality around me was something I had zero control over. In fact, at the time, I had no control over anything, including myself. I decided I wanted to change.

Day by day, I'd practice deep breathing and meditation, both at home before work and even a bit while I was driving. I consciously tried to relax while driving and reminded myself that traffic was out of my control. After nearly a year of practice, I remember being in heavy traffic and running late to work, which was the perfect trigger situation for me, but I wasn't freaking out. I wasn't stressed at all. I just thought to myself, *I guess I'll be a little late.* It was at that moment I realized what had happened. I had re-trained myself to be calm when there was traffic.

This shift happened not only concerning traffic but in other areas of my life as well. I got a little more comfortable with being uncomfortable. I began to accept that life would never be exactly as I envisioned it, so I stopped fighting with myself so much. I felt much more at ease. The most interesting thing about this personal antidote is how things have gone my way more frequently since I let go of trying to control everything.

When I speak about being uncomfortable and how important it is to get used to it to some degree, I'm reminded again of a child having a temper tantrum. Most adults would say to a child, "You can't get your way all the time." But the funny thing is, as adults, we expect things to go as we want them to, everything from traffic parting for us, to getting a promotion, to wanting others to behave in a certain way. Most of us, whether we realize it or not, have some deep conscious and unconscious control issues. It's okay. It doesn't mean you're a bad person. The desire to control life is rooted in fear: a lack of trust that things will work out as they're meant to and that we will learn lessons along the way. Sometimes we will win. Sometimes we will lose. If you want to be more skillful in life, learning to accept that life will sometimes be uncomfortable is a must.

Transition

So much of life is made up of spaces in between: in between jobs, in between relationships, in between stages of childhood or child-rearing. Everything is a transition on our journey between life and death. Yet, change is something that we struggle with most. Many people come to my counseling practice when they are having trouble adjusting during times of transition.

> *People have a hard time letting go of their suffering. Out of a fear of the unknown, they prefer suffering that is familiar.*[16]
> ~ *Thich Nhat Hanh*

Sometimes, we might choose to stay stuck in a relationship, in a job, in a circumstance, or we are simply stuck in inaction. We are so afraid to make the wrong decision that we just stay with the discomfort we are currently feeling. Transition is an uncomfortable experience, yet it defines life: change from one form, state, style, or place to another.

Whether we like it or not, we are constantly changing. We are all aging. Those around us are as well, and in the aging process, our bodies, minds, and emotions all shift. Our life circumstances change from one year to another, sometimes from one week or one day to another. Yet, most of us tend to try to cling to one moment, one way of being, or one perspective.

I've always turned to nature when I find myself mentally or emotionally stuck during a time of transition. Trees are such a beautiful reminder that everything changes. We can watch as they grow tiny buds on their branches, blossom with a full mane of green leaves, and then, as those leaves dry, change color and drop. We can see them stand proud even when they're bare and have lost everything. What a great metaphor for a human life. We will all cycle through our own seasons of growth and loss and everything in between. The question is, how do you want to show up during your transitions?

We can be dragged by life, kicking, screaming, and whining, or we can try to move forward with intention and grace. Life will urge us onward regardless of what we do. Moving through transition with intention doesn't mean that you won't grieve, feel, or give yourself time to rest. It means that you won't dwell there for too long but rather draw on your strengths, your values, and your goals and keep going. Take some time to reflect on how you've previously experienced transition in your life before and consider whether you're happy with the process. What might you do the same in your next transition, and what might you want to shift?

Doubt: The Voice in Your Head

You know what I'm talking about unless you haven't slowed down enough to observe it. We all have a voice of doubt inside. It's the internal "demon" that tells us we aren't good enough or that we can't do something. It's the voice that tries to tell us we aren't lovable or that we must always be at our absolute best, and if we ever make a mistake, we won't be loved, but we will be abandoned. It is not a voice of truth, though it may try to convince you it is. This voice comes from our past, from cruel words that have hurt us, from mistakes we've made and perhaps been ridiculed for, or from other circumstances that have cultivated shame and doubt. We all have this inner voice to varying degrees. It's important to practice observing yours to truly understand just how loud or how mean it is. And then, you can practice setting it aside with a simple label.

When I catch myself hooked into this inner demon, I try to pause and say to myself, *That's just the voice of doubt*. This helps me not take it to heart but see more clearly that it is just part of the darkness inside of me. I need to look at it, but I don't have to believe it or make choices based on it. In fact, I will often purposefully tell myself the opposite of this voice to try to bring myself to a neutral center. From there, I can use intellect to cite evidence either supporting or denying the doubt concept, or I can use my deeper instinct and intuition to access an inner knowing that is more powerful than the emotional and dramatic voice of doubt. I recommend trying this for yourself now or, perhaps, moving on to explore this concept more deeply in the ego and soul section below.

Trauma

A traumatic event is often described as a situation that lacks predictability, safety, and personal control. Lots can fall into this category. Trauma may, but doesn't have to involve serious, life-threatening circumstances that are physically or emotionally violent. For some, big life changes are traumatic: moving, losing a job, losing a loved one, breaking up with a spouse, lover, or friend, or being publicly embarrassed in some way.

Here, we will return to the concept of post-traumatic stress as opposed to post-traumatic growth. We all perceive things differently, and some of us are wired to experience stressful events with greater intensity. This is not a character flaw or in any way your fault, and my intention is certainly not to make you feel ashamed about the way you experience difficulty. It is, however, important to acknowledge, understand, and see reality clearly so you can begin on a path toward healing.

- What have you experienced in your life that was traumatic, that lacked predictability, safety, and control? Take a moment to reflect on this or journal about it.

- How did you experience these traumatic events in your life?

- Did you sweep them under the metaphorical carpet, in essence burying them in your psyche in the hope that they never emerge again?

- Did you grieve the situation and eventually move forward?

- Does the situation still haunt you; does it enter your mind regularly, impacting your daily life, especially when something triggers the memory?

- After healing from the situation, did you become inspired or driven to help others or engage in something positive to help you move forward?

Our ability to process trauma is complex. There is some evidence that if your parents experienced high levels of trauma and stress in their lives, you could be more predisposed to anxiety, depression, and PTSD.[17] There are also other psychological predictors of your capacity for trauma, including how many early childhood traumas you experienced (ACE or adverse childhood experiences assessment).[18] What's important to remember is that with time, effort, mindfulness, and sometimes therapy, you can shift your capacity for managing traumatic events, and you can heal and move forward from past ones. Awareness is key.

These questions may help you develop greater self-awareness:

- When do you feel safe, and what do you require in order to feel safe? This might not be an easy answer, but it's important to consider.

- How can you accept the fact that you cannot change your past? Does this require forgiveness of yourself and of those who harmed you? (Refer to the Care part of this book for a definition of forgiveness and practices that support).

The practices of compassion and gratitude help retrain the brain to see differently, and they can help you heal. Review Part One: Mindfulness for practices and Part Three: Care for further recommendations. Please remember to go slowly and be gentle with yourself on a path of healing from trauma. Sometimes, you might need to gently nudge yourself forward, but try to maintain a neutral or positive inner voice. Try to release the tension and anger you are feeling regarding a particular circumstance, as they can only cause you harm.

Stress

We've been discussing stress in various ways on these last several pages, and we each need to recognize and understand our capacity for challenging circumstances and life events. Allostatic load is a term that was coined in 1993 by Bruce McEwen and Eliot Stellar, referring to the cumulative effect of chronic stress on physical, mental, and emotional health. When our stressors consistently outweigh our ability to cope with them, we experience chronic stress, which has significant wear and tear on the body over time. We must realize this and not sweep it under the rug of distraction. Know when you are at your capacity. Then, level up your coping strategies.

How do you recognize that you're stressed? Do you feel it in your jaw, your shoulders, or your belly? Do you deny that you experience stress, chalking it up to being tough? Do you wait until someone else mentions that you seem stressed or until you overreact to something small because you just can't take one more thing? Consider how you cope with stress and what practices you regularly do to make yourself feel better.

We've been lulled into believing that sitting and watching videos is stress management, but it's actually distraction and avoidance. While sometimes we might want to be entertained or to step away from our stressors in avoidance, it is a concern if that is your only "stress-management" practice. Electronic media is not a mindful way to release stress from your body, emotions, or mind. The problem is that we live in a quick-fix world, and watching even a five-minute distracting cat video on YouTube might *feel* like stress management, at least for a moment, but there are other, more effective ways to deal with stress. Part Three: Care will explore meditation, exercise, time in nature, face-to-face time with loved ones, time for hobbies, these practices, and more. Remember, when you feel short on time because you are so stressed, that's when you need to take extra time to do self-care, as counterintuitive as this might seem. In my experience, many people report getting more done and feeling less stressed when they up their stress management strategies during busy periods.

Your Ego & Your Soul

Part of the process of getting to know yourself and learning to embrace yourself in all your neurosis is understanding that you are a multidimensional being. Your physical self, your energy, your breath, your mind and emotions, your wisdom, your bliss, and your best, most true self, it's all you. It's important to recognize this and understand that parts of you cover, divide, and block you from your higher self.

Think of it like this: the soul is at your center, your core. It's who you are deep inside, the best, most connected, divine part of you, that is always compassionate, loving, wise, and joyful. There's no stress in the soul, just calm, warmth, curiosity, and awe at each moment of experience. Peace is at your core.

And then there's life. You experience disappointment, trauma, mistreatment, and abuse. You struggle, worry, fear, and replay the past in your mind. You grieve and create layers of protection, thinking that if you metaphorically cover your most vulnerable and pure self, you will avoid pain and suffering in the future. The only problem with this (ego) thinking is that if you cover yourself to avoid pain, you're also numbing yourself to joy because you're covering the part of yourself that's most able to access that deep connection to life, your soul.

If you're following this line of thinking, join me in going one step further. Think about each human life as a moving car with two drivers (or two perspectives). One perspective is the ego, and one perspective is the soul. These two entities mirror the concepts of fear and love. Fear/Ego tells us to avoid life; it is dangerous, and we could get hurt. Love/Soul tells us to open our arms and embrace it all with compassion and curiosity. The question then becomes, who do you want to drive you through life? Do you want your ego in the driver's seat? Maybe if you're negotiating a business deal or getting propositioned in a bar, yes, you need your ego in the driver's seat to help you be safe and protected. But if you're considering your purpose in life, an intuitive career change, helping other human beings, or confronting the prospect of love, do you want your ego in the driver's seat or your soul? In many circumstances, we could use a little more guidance from the soul, but we allow fear and the ego to bully us into submission. So, how can we learn to *choose* who drives our human vehicle? Try this exercise (offered by Steve Treu, author of *New Eyes*).

Contemplate your ego and your soul/best self. Think about how these two parts interact or take the lead in your choices and actions.

To help cultivate greater awareness and choice, consider giving a name to your "soul self." Your ego self is the name of the human body you were given at birth.

To give a name to your soul, think about what's meaningful to you, a metaphor, a story, or a wise relative, and create a name that conjures positive, loving, compassionate energy.

Once you've named your soul, put this into practice by asking yourself, when faced with upset, irritation, or even a simple choice, *what would <soul name> have to say about this?* Or, *Am I acting from <soul name> or <my name/ego>?*[19]

Example: my ego name is Joni. My soul's name (that I chose) is Shiva. So, I might ask myself, in an annoying circumstance, is it Joni who is upset about this? What would Shiva think?

It's a fun, awareness-building exercise to help you peel off the layers that cover your best self, making it available when you need it the most.

Finding Meaning

What is life asking of you? I can't tell you the meaning of your life, no more than you can tell me mine. It is the life work of each of us to ask ourselves the right questions and explore the answers without getting caught up in over-questioning and over-analyzing. We must take action in life, or it will pass us by. Herein lies our challenge. To some degree, we need to contemplate. To be quiet. To listen. To figure ourselves out. But we are limited on time; life is finite whether we think about it or not. So, we have to practice balance between patience and action. We might not always have the right answers, and we might not always choose the right action, and that's okay. Remember that being on a path of exploration is more important than feeling like you have all the exact answers. There should be an ebb and flow to meaning-making, a life-long journey of experimenting and exploring with curiosity and patience. For many people, considering what is beyond our daily grind is a way of finding meaning.

All life is an experiment. The more experiments you make, the better.
~ Ralph Waldo Emerson [20]

Spirituality

Spirituality is different from religion, and while they can coincide, they don't have to. Religion is often how we are introduced to the concepts of spirituality (that which relates to our soul or higher self), but sometimes, we step outside the confines of a religious framework to feel, wonder, and learn on our own. Where are you on your path of spirituality and religion?

I know some religiously devout individuals who are quite spiritual. They have found truth in their practices and the faith in which they were raised or the faith they have embraced as adults. They feel authentic, connected to something greater, and at peace with life. What a beautiful thing! I've also met some atheists who have found meaning in their daily lives, live with values and morals, meditate with a community, feel purpose, and savor every moment they have. How wonderful for them! There are also some people I work with who are lost somewhere on the spectrum of believing something but not quite sure what. They've stepped away from the religion they were raised with for varied reasons but haven't found a path forward and feel empty or lost. Sometimes, these individuals aren't even interested in exploring anything concerning spirituality. They don't feel it would help them, so they avoid contemplation in this area of life. However, spirituality and meaning are core pieces of human wellness and flourishing. So again, I ask, what do you believe, and how much time do you devote to exploring your sense of spirituality? Can you even define it for yourself?

How much time do you or have you spent reading "wisdom texts"? The Bible, Yoga Sutras, Tao Te Ching, Bhagavad Gita, poetry by Rumi, philosophy by Nietzsche, Stoicism, Greek philosophy, the Dhammapada, or others? These texts have been read by millions of people over hundreds or even thousands of years for a reason: they offer insight into the human condition, how to cope, how to have a broader perspective, and how to connect with what one might refer to as spirituality.

You might ask yourself, *how do I make sense of texts like these?* It's important to remember that these kinds of texts are generally written in metaphor with lessons attached to them, kind of like Aesop's fables. Many people may enjoy the literal aspects of these texts, but they may not be able to make sense of them on a deeper level. Or they may not understand or appreciate them at all and throw the whole text out or write off any possible value it might contain. The answer to deriving meaning from spiritual texts lies in taking it one step at a time, using your own lens of understanding and belief. You can make meaning from any one of these spiritual texts, and I'll give you an example to show you how. Then, I challenge you to pick up one of these books, read a bit of it, and try to do the same. Here's a well-known psalm from The Old Testament and how I interpret it and relate to it.

Psalm 23

The Lord is my shepherd, I shall not want.
He maketh me to lie down in green pastures. He leadeth me beside still waters. He restoreth my soul.
He leadeth me on a path of righteousness for His name's sake.
Yay, though I walk through the valley of the shadow of death, I shall fear no evil, for thou art with me.
Thy rod and my staff comfort me.
Thou preparest a table before me in the presence of mine enemies.
Thou anointest my head with oil.
My cup runneth over.
Surely goodness and mercy shall follow me all the days of my life, and I will dwell in the house of the Lord forever.

I was raised in a casually Christian-ish household that was very open to broad interpretations of spirituality from multiple religions and other sources, not just Christianity alone. As I grew into adulthood, I studied yoga philosophy, Hinduism, Buddhism, and more. I sought out people to discuss various perspectives and beliefs so I could make sense of what I felt in my heart, mind, and soul. Therefore, when I read Psalm 23, I process it through my lens, and I'm encouraging you to do so as well. Here's what I see and feel from this beautiful psalm.

The first line of the psalm states, *The Lord is my shepherd, I shall not want.*
In this line, I interpret the message as: I need to trust that God (the universe or life) is guiding me for a reason. I am here in this circumstance to learn and grow from whatever happens, so don't worry. In this context, the shepherd is a guide so I can feel protected, not alone.

Next, *He maketh me to lie down in green pastures. He leadeth me beside still waters. He restoreth my soul.*
Here, I am being reminded to be in the present moment. Be still. Connect with nature. Watch how nature handles the passage of time and change. Let that be my guide to restore me in a deep way. Don't worry too much, stress too much, overthink, or overwork. Remember to rest and enjoy life. This will brighten

how I feel inside and restore my soul.

He leadeth me on a path of righteousness for His name's sake.
Since this is the Old Testament, I know the psalmist is referring to God himself. The psalm says, look, God is showing you an example here. Follow this lead. Do this, practice these kinds of values and morals, and you'll be fulfilled, happy, and create a community.

Yay, though I walk through the valley of the shadow of death, I shall fear no evil, for thou art with me.
In ancient texts, death didn't always refer to literal death but to change. When I experience big changes, marriage, divorce, children, loss, and job changes, I experience the symbolic death of one thing as I move into a different stage. We are always walking in this valley of the shadow of change, and yes, life is limited. I don't have forever. So I shouldn't waste it being fearful. Live life to the fullest and trust that the universe (God or life) has me, holds me, and will help guide me to make the best choices if I pay attention. I am not alone.

Thy rod and my staff comfort me.
This is a reminder that I am being guided if I relax and pay attention. It'll be okay.

Thou preparest a table before me in the presence of mine enemies.
I love this line. Preparing a table, as if for a feast, in the presence of enemies, I believe, is another way of saying that God/the universe/life has your back. And I believe it also refers to the idea that I can be my own worst enemy. So how can I sit for dinner with my worst enemy when it's me? Remember the story I mentioned earlier in the book about inviting your demons to tea instead of resisting them? In that story, the woman says to her demons, "You've been here before; you'll be here again, so why not sit for tea." Sitting for tea or for a feast is a way of feeding my demons and my inner enemies at the root of my insecurity, which is what my inner enemy is. It's not fueling the enemy but rather feeding what is being starved inside of me. What is being starved feels lost, scared, tender, and can lash out — the essence of my inner enemy. What a beautiful and comforting line - to prepare a table to feed what is empty inside.

Thou anointest my head with oil.
This refers to a blessing. Once again, a reminder to let go of fear and remember that I've got this.

My cup runneth over.
A statement of positive psychology! Even though I might be struggling right now, I think of the things I can be grateful for because it is guaranteed that in some area of life, my cup runneth over and I have everything I need.

Surely goodness and mercy shall follow me all the days of my life, and I will dwell in the house of the Lord forever.
A final reminder that it's all going to be okay. That statement doesn't mean I will always get what I want, but that I will get what I need in order to learn, grow, and have the potential to be the best version of myself. It's a reminder that we are all in this together, with other human beings, in the same "house." And that life, the universe, or God, is always looking out for us. This pattern of growth is always available to me in some form, as energy is neither created nor destroyed, but it just changes form. So, whatever one's spiritual belief, there's a cycle that happens, and we are a part of it. I can trust that and not worry so much.

Did my interpretation of Psalm 23 resonate with you? It's okay if it did, and it's okay if it didn't. What's most important is that you learn to read bits of these ancient texts, filter out what doesn't make sense, hold on to what does make sense, and try to find a nugget of wisdom in everything you explore. That is how you can dive deeply into spirituality and feel connected. This can help you refresh your current religious practices, expand your current spiritual beliefs, or set you on a path toward greater clarity for yourself and what resonates with you.

With this goal in mind, here's a well-known passage from The Bhagavad Gita (18:47):

> *It is better to strive in one's own dharma than to succeed in the dharma of another. Nothing is ever lost in following one's own dharma, but competition in another's dharma breeds fear and insecurity.*

In this passage, Krishna is speaking to Arjuna and those of us who read the words. He is saying that we have to figure out our own meaning and path in life (dharma). No one can give us the answers; it doesn't work like that. Although someone can serve as a guide and perhaps say things that resonate with us, we still have to do the work of looking inside, exploring who we are and what's going on. Then, we can start to break down the things that aren't working and grow into new ways of thinking, feeling, and taking action in life. If we don't do this work, if we avoid it, or try to take shortcuts, following someone else's path, we won't be happy. It won't feel right. And we are wasting our precious time.

Time is all we have, and as the famous Tibetan Buddhist master Milarepa reminded his students in the Eleventh-Century, "Without being mindful of death, whatever Dharma practices you take up will be merely superficial."[21] We have to find meaning and live it daily while we can. The philosophical school of Stoicism, which flourished in ancient Greece and Rome, was well known for saying *memento mori*, or remember death. These words of wisdom, as well as Milarepa's sentiment, are not meant to be dark, morbid, or depressing but rather to inspire us to remember that we could die at any moment. If this were our last day, would we waste time being frustrated over the little things that are outside of our control? Would we hold a grudge against a loved one with whom we argued? Would we want to live these last hours with meanness or with kindness? Think how Ebenezer Scrooge changed after being shown his life from the perspective of *memento mori*. For each of us, seeking our self, our truth, and our path is our work, day in and day out, if we choose it.

Thirteenth-Century Sufi poet and scholar Rumi provides insight into his spiritual journey when he tells us,

> *I looked for myself and found only God. I looked for God and found only myself.*

Do you have space to access your spirituality? Have you found a literal space to practice? This is important. Consider whether you feel connected to something greater when you are in church, in nature, in solitude, or somewhere else. Take the time to be present and allow yourself to consider something beyond your daily tasks and to-do lists.

Values & Ethics

What are your values and morals? You might think you know what your values and morals are, but perhaps you can't answer that question easily. Research shows that those who live in alignment with their virtues are happier, so I encourage you to write your own personal set of ethics and values. Sometimes, studying other sets of morals, ethics, and values is helpful as you start this process. Pay attention to what resonates with you and why it's important. Then, consider how to apply that value in your life. Let's begin by looking at various religious, spiritual, and philosophical traditions.

Explore the Ten Commandments from the Old Testament (remember to tease apart the meanings of these to make them resonate with you):

1. You shall have no other gods before Me.
2. You shall not make idols.
3. You shall not take the name of the Lord your God in vain.
4. Remember the Sabbath day to keep it holy.
5. Honor your father and your mother.
6. You shall not murder.
7. You shall not commit adultery.
8. You shall not steal.
9. You shall not bear false witness against your neighbor.
10. You shall not covet.

Or try the Yamas and Niyamas from the Yoga Sutras:

Yamas

- Ahimsa (non-harming or non-violence in thought, word and deed)
- Satya (truthfulness)
- Asteya (non-stealing)
- Brahmacharya (celibacy or 'right use of energy')
- Aparigraha (non-greed or non-hoarding)

Niyamas

- Saucha (cleanliness)
- Santosha (contentment)
- Tapas (discipline)
- Svadhyaya (study of the self and of wisdom texts)
- Isvara Pranidhana (surrender to a higher being or contemplation of a higher power)

They sound similar to the Ten Commandments, don't they?

In Judaism, the Torah, the Hebrew Scriptures, and the Talmud emphasize embodying the following values:

- Compassion
- Peace
- Human dignity
- Integrity
- Justice
- Industriousness

The Muslim faith adheres to the Five Core Pillars of Islam:

- Shahada (the creed of belief)
- Salah (daily prayers)
- Zakat (giving to people experiencing poverty)
- Sawm (fasting during Ramadan)
- Hajj (pilgrimage to Mecca)

The Stoic philosophy has four central values:

- Wisdom: defined as common sense, calculation, quick-wittedness, discretion, and resourcefulness
- Justice: qualities of honesty, equity, and fair dealing
- Courage: moving through challenges with endurance and resilience
- Moderation: acting with restraint, self-control, and discipline

Some people like to express what's most important to them:

- Family
- Faith
- Service to others
- Travel

My moral code (and how I define and apply these concepts) is as follows:

- Connection:
    - I will connect with myself through meditation and exploration of spirituality.
    - I will connect with others in my life — creating deep, meaningful relationships by listening and being present with them.
- Care:
    - I will care for my body as it is my temple by eating healthfully, exercising, meditating, and taking time for myself and my needs.
    - I will care gently for those I love in the ways they need me to.
- Kindness:
    - I will practice kindness and compassion towards myself when I misstep.
    - I will be kind towards others, under the positive assumption that everyone is trying their best. I will try not to cause harm to any others.
- Composure:
    - I will practice ease and letting go, trying not to sweat the small stuff.
    - I will be a dependable, solid friend, partner, therapist, teacher, and mentor.
    - I will hold space for any challenging circumstance with calm, open composure.
- Skillfulness:
    - I will utilize my practice of mindfulness and choose the best

course of action as I can, moment to moment.

- - I will be honest in all circumstances, tempering it with kindness.

- - I will continually try to communicate clearly and succinctly.

- - I will listen to others closely, with full attention.

- Growth:

- - I will continue on a path of learning and will always try to be a better version of myself tomorrow than I am today while still accepting myself in each moment as a flawed human with the best of intentions. I will practice all of these qualities listed here with focus and gentle determination.

- Patience:

- - I will practice remembering that circumstances unfold in time, not on my schedule. I will be patient with myself when I make mistakes. I will sit with impatience, hold it gently, and breathe until the tension passes.

- Trust:

- - I will surrender when I feel resistance so I don't end up metaphorically beating my head against a wall. I will instead try to find the lesson in every circumstance under the positive assumption that it is happening for a reason. I will try to cultivate trust that all will be as it should be.

What can you draw on from all these values, morals, and ethics when you filter them through your beliefs, your life, and what's important to you? What's missing here that is vital to you and how you want to live? Reflect on this and consider writing your own moral code, a set of five to ten statements you wish to live by. You could start from scratch or draw on what I've offered above from the various traditions.

Remember not just to pick a word like "kindness" and leave it at that. As I demonstrated above, contemplate what kindness means to you and how you intend to put it into action in your life. Morals and values aren't useful unless you apply them. They are intended to be a compass to guide you in everything from interactions with your family and friends to your actions at work to how you handle a moral dilemma. Knowing and practicing your values will help you find purpose and meaning in your life because you are always working toward embodying those characteristics. Consider keeping your moral code on your phone, a piece of laminated paper in your wallet, or posting it somewhere in your home where you are reminded of it frequently.

Intention Mantra / Motto

Along with your values, ethics, and moral code, it can be helpful to add a personal creed, motto, or intention mantra. This is a word, a few words, or a short phrase that you can use during meditation or simply throughout your day to remind yourself of your intentions. For instance, my long-time personal mantra is *peace and patience*. These are two qualities I find I need to practice on an ongoing basis, and if you read my moral code, you'll see how they relate to several values I hold dear and want to live by. Repeating them alongside my breath for a few minutes in the morning can help direct me into a positive mindset for the day. After you write your moral code, consider what you want to focus on specifically or perhaps what you struggle with implementing the most. Then, write yourself a positive mantra to remind you of how you want to live. Your mantra might always be the same, or it might be something that changes over time. It can be very personal; it's not something you ever have to share with anyone. However, sharing this process and encouraging it in others is essential if you're in a leadership role. It will improve everyone's individual experience and collective interactions if your team (or family) embodies its own personal code daily.

Final Discovery Questions

With all this in mind: your koshas, your strengths, your intelligence, your fear, your stress, your spirituality, your morals, who are you? Are you a conglomeration of all these pieces? Pause for another few breaths. Inhale… Exhale… Slow it down and close your eyes. Open your eyes and ask yourself these questions, either pausing to ponder or writing out your responses. Try to answer them for yourself before moving on to the Care section:

- Who am I?

- What are my strengths?

- What are my negative patterns and growth edges?

- Where am I out of balance?

- What are my primary values and morals?

- What do I believe and trust in?

- What do I *need* in life right now?

- What do I *want* in life right now?

- What do I *really* want at a deep level?

Part Three: Care

(Self-Care)

Think of a tree in your backyard. She reaches with deep roots, drawing water from the earth, carrying this essential component of life to her leaves, where photosynthesis takes place. She opens to receive the sunlight and feed herself, exchanging oxygen for carbon dioxide. She buds in spring, grows vibrant through the summer, and then allows her leaves to fade and let go in fall. They drop to the ground where they can nourish the soil around her so she can continue to draw nutrients from the earth as she stands proud and bare throughout a cold winter. This is the cycle of a tree in each year of its life. Because we are interconnected, each tree's self-care is beneficial to us all. Trees provide us with oxygen, shade, beauty, and shelter. But what if a tree began to resist this natural process of self-fueling? What if she resisted photosynthesis or dropping leaves in the winter? Well, she wouldn't be able to sustain herself or be of benefit to the forest or those around her.

The necessity of human self-care isn't just a modern platitude. It's a way of fueling yourself so that you can have the energy and capacity to meet challenges, make skillful decisions, cultivate inner growth, make space for happiness and gratitude, and help others, too. On a very basic level, we are like the tree. If we flow with the cycles of life without resistance and care for ourselves (especially during cold, dark winters) we can fulfill our purpose more effectively, be of service to others, and be at peace.

To use another metaphor, we are like a vessel filled with water. We are the vessel or cup, and the water is the energy we have. If we are constantly pouring from our cup (at work, with family, friends, children, parents, pets, home, and everything else that demands energy expenditure), eventually we are going to be empty (use all our water/energy). If we continue to pour from an empty cup, we are trying to give what we don't have. We become short-tempered, resentful, exhausted, and grumpy. Ever feel that way? It's a path to compassion fatigue and burnout.

You can feel stronger, happier, more helpful, more alive, and align with your values better if you learn how to fuel yourself in multiple ways, in each layer of your being. So, in Part Three: Care, we are revisiting the koshas as they relate to various self-care practices: for your physical self, energetic self, mental/emotional self, wisdom, and bliss. There will be some overlap, as many practices that are good for our minds/emotions are also good for our bodies. In other words, that which offers wisdom can also heal the mind and emotions, etc. Remember that self-care is about striking a balance between nurturing ourselves and challenging ourselves. Self-care is not all about massages and vacations; it also involves hard work.

It is not my intention to make you feel bad for all the things you aren't doing, but rather to offer you a wide array of practices you can choose from and start to incorporate, little by little.

As I've mentioned before, perspective is everything, right? If you look at self-care and immediately think, *oh great, something else to put on my to-do list*, consider that these practices will help you make your to-do list more purposeful and enable you to get it done with greater ease. This will happen because you'll be filling your cup with energy, clarity, and calm composure. You'll be fueling yourself, creating your own kind of photosynthesis, so you can have the vitality for more skillful action, as opposed to worry-ridden, scattered reaction or the inaction of being stuck. Self-care makes for greater physical, mental, and emotional health and well-being. The tips I offer here for self-care are based on my years of training in physical health and wellness, mental and emotional health, and spiritual/wisdom growth practices. They're also based on my own personal experience and the experience of my clients.

We've talked about habits before, and I want to remind you that sticking with self-care practices is also habit-based. To help you strike a balance between gentleness and kick-yourself-into-gear motivation, consider the cycle of change model created by James Prochaska and Carlo DiClemente. They state that there are six stages of change.

- Pre-contemplation: There is no intention to change behavior.

- Contemplation: You are aware a problem exists, but there's no commitment to action.

- Preparation: There's intent on taking action to address the issue.

- Action: Active modification of behavior.

- Maintenance: Sustained change, where new behavior replaces old behavior.

- Relapse: Falling back to old patterns of behavior.[22]

It is common to cycle through these stages in an upward spiral a few times before something is successfully integrated as a new, habitual pattern of behavior, and you stay in the "maintenance" stage. Everyone's a little different in that regard, so be mindful and notice what stage you're in and how you feel about it. Applaud yourself for what you're already doing and consider what else you might add in over time. What would it require for you to take action? Remember that you can learn to care for yourself deeply, no matter where you start. Also, remember that change is hard, and if you have experienced complicated circumstances or trauma, be gentle with yourself and your expectations. Find a healthy balance between tapas and gentleness. Try to avoid extreme, all-or-nothing perspectives or practices. That kind of attitude tends to lead toward either burnout or avoidance.

Learning new ways to care for yourself and implementing such practices in a balanced way encourages cognitive flexibility or adaptive brain training, which can help you be open to new circumstances and ideas. You'll benefit from this growth in both the short and long term. Your kosha layers will become healthier, and you'll connect more easily to your deeper layers. You'll feel better overall, and you'll respond to future challenges with more ease. This is because you will be learning how to successfully navigate the process of deep listening regarding your own needs and building the capacity to fulfill them, regardless of your circumstances. You'll be learning how to create the experience of equanimity, and that inner strength and resilience will change your life for the better.

While working through the tips here, or when working through any self-improvement program, seek out a support system both within yourself and beyond, perhaps connecting with a good friend, significant other, or coach to help keep you on track. It's easy to fall back to laziness or complacency until habits are formed and you experience the results. Keep checking in with yourself. Try asking yourself regularly, is what I'm doing inspiring growth, distraction, or destruction?

Mindful awareness of the koshas offers insight into what you need. This creates growth, as does incorporating healthy habits. We aren't growing when we are on autopilot or in a state of distraction: watching TV, surfing the Internet or social media, playing video games, or constantly moving from one activity to the next, staying "busy." Doing anything too much or too little can become a distraction, even over-exercising, over-educating yourself, or being so much of a health nut you never allow yourself to enjoy pleasurable things. If done in excess, these behaviors can be self-destructive. Of course, there are more obvious destructive and addictive practices like overeating, drinking too much, using drugs or other substances, and even zoning out for days binge-watching a show is a destructive habit. Remember, we have limited time here. How do you want to use your time and your life span?

Attending to Your Physical Body

Our physical body is the home of our mind, our emotions, our soul. Cultivating balance here will change your life. Perhaps you already eat well and exercise, or perhaps you don't pay much attention to your physical body. The following tips will help you shift your perspective to one of true self-care, not self-abuse. There is no need to starve yourself, exercise to the point of injury, or mentally beat yourself up. When we talk about care, it is just that: how to nourish and fine-tune your vessel.

Physical Stress Release

We hold stress in our physical bodies, not just on a daily basis but accumulatively throughout our lives. The trauma we experience can get stuck in our bodies as tightness and tension and even create illness. There's a branch of psychotherapy called somatic therapy, which addresses the connections between the mind and the body, using both talk therapy and physical practices to create holistic healing.

Here are some practices you can do regularly to help the release of stress from your body:

Stretching

Whether you do yoga, which incorporates strengthening and stretching with breathing, or if you just stretch all the major muscle groups in your body, stretching offers profound results. In addition to relieving physical muscle tension, you enhance the performance of your muscles, decrease your risk of injury, increase blood flow, expand your range of motion, and even improve your posture.

Movement

I could refer to this as "exercise," but I've learned that word can bring groans and eyerolls. However, exercise is just about moving your body. Long ago, people didn't exercise; rather, they did physical labor that involved moving their bodies, lifting heavy objects, and elevating heart rates through faster-paced activities. These activities weren't labeled as exercise; people were just doing what they needed to, and it involved physical movement.

In today's sedentary culture, where so many of us work at desks all day and then go home to sit in front of the television, we now have a practice called "exercise" where we mimic the sorts of things that people used to do naturally. Of course, we've added some modern concepts regarding physical movement as we've learned about health and balance in the physical body.

Walking is a perfect movement activity. It requires nothing but a comfortable pair of shoes and perhaps appropriate gear to walk in inclement weather. You can easily build stamina and strength by walking up hills or varying your speed. Remember to incorporate stretching to maintain or increase your range of motion.

Go to a gym if you prefer. Use elliptical machines, bikes, treadmills, and weights. Use your body weight. Dance. Try classes or exercise on your own. Be open to trying different practices to find something you not only enjoy but something that challenges you.

Being Uncomfortable

The body is reflective of the mind and vice versa. If you are in a state of chronic stress, you might feel like you are already at maximum capacity, and extra physical effort might feel impossible or even painful. To cultivate steadiness in both mind and body, however, we must challenge ourselves, which isn't always easy. Remember that discomfort doesn't always mean danger. Growth can require us to be uncomfortable, as I've said before. When we practice being at ease with discomfort, we increase our capacity for life and all the painful things that can happen because we can tolerate them more easily.

This is not exactly a "no pain, no gain" mentality. It is gentler and more mindful than that. In an ancient wisdom text called The Yoga Sūtras of Patañjali, there's a concept that emphasizes this very idea: *sthira* and *sukha* are the Sanskrit words that refer to the balance between effort and ease.

Most of us tend toward either more effort, pushing ourselves to the point of exhaustion or injury, or toward more ease, telling ourselves we can't do something tough and not trying very hard. Magic happens in the middle, between strength and softness, control and surrender, sthira and sukha. Allow the experience of being uncomfortable to challenge you to find the fine line between the two and practice there. Ultimately, if you can do this with your physical practices, you'll find it's easier to balance mentally and emotionally.

When I started the physical poses of yoga, I wanted to push myself hard into some demanding positions. *Bakasana*, or crow pose, was one that I wanted to conquer. I'd try to hurl myself up, hold my breath, push and squeeze, and I'd always fall. It wasn't until I learned how to breathe, focus, and be calm that I was able to exert the right amount of effort to ease into the pose and hold it with a degree of challenging comfort. Not coincidentally, I soon found myself breathing and being calm in challenging work situations while dealing with difficult people. The physical had been transmitted into my mental-emotional-behavioral realm without me consciously making an effort. So don't be afraid to challenge yourself physically. Discomfort doesn't mean danger. It's okay for things to be hard. Do it anyway and relax into the process as best you can. It's a valuable life lesson you can apply throughout various areas of your life.

Tense and Release

Here's a simple practice that can help you relieve physical stress, sometimes within just a minute or so. It's called progressive muscle relaxation. Scan your body slowly and pause your attention at each part, breathing in and tensing that area, then when you breathe out, sigh and relax the area. You can start at the feet and work your way up to your head, or vice versa. Try just taking a few breaths where you inhale and tense everything, then exhale and relax everything. This simple practice can help to soften tight muscles and release stress that might otherwise get bound up in the physical body. Try it a few times a day, and remember to incorporate your breath as it cues the nervous system that it's okay to let go.

Massage

I highly recommend budgeting so that you can get a professional massage either monthly or every other month. If that just isn't possible, perhaps you can trade massages with your significant other or best friend. Massage can help to loosen tight muscles, but more than that, it elicits a relaxation response in the body, lowering heart rate, blood pressure, and stress hormones. Massage can even boost immune function (stimulating the lymphatic system) and mental sharpness (by improving circulation and relieving fatigue). If you've never gotten a professional massage, you might be a little nervous, but think of it as you would a doctor's appointment. You're working with a trained professional to understand the body and promote relaxation. In some cultures, massage is a part of health and wellness, and everyone gets a massage regularly from infancy. During the COVID-19 pandemic and the resulting social distancing, we realized more than ever what a crucial role touch plays in our well-being. In recent years, studies have shown that tender touch can reduce stress hormones and boost mood. Massage can offer this if you don't otherwise have it in your life. This is definitely one of the more pleasant and easier self-care practices to incorporate, so remind yourself that you are worth it and schedule a massage.

Sexuality

Speaking of more pleasant self-care practices, let's explore sexuality as self-care. If you have a partner, you can access the healing power of touch along with a mental-emotional connection, feelings of intimacy, and perhaps the physical release of an orgasm, which can boost mood, reduce pain, and help you sleep better. Even if you're alone, you can still enjoy your sexuality. It's good for you! Yet, there can be issues around sex that hold you back, such as insecurity or physical inhibition resulting from negative experiences, trauma, or conditioned shame around the pleasure of sex. It is a natural part of life, and we are built to enjoy it. Consider your sexuality and how it fits into your life, your values, and your schedule. Look at it as cherished self-care for your body, mind, and spirit, as well as tender care for your sweetheart if you are in a healthy relationship.

Although your values and feelings around sex are what's most important, remember that sex with another person is an energy exchange. Who are you sharing your energy with, and how? Is it nourishing for you, or are there negative feelings that accompany the experience? Take the time to allow yourself to feel the experience and be present with the after-effects. Your body, mind, and emotions are sacred to be honored in this way. Notice if you avoid acknowledging or exploring your experience. Talk to your partner or find resources that help cultivate conversation and connection around sex.

Body Fuel

Our bodies require nourishment not only to survive but to thrive. Unfortunately, the typical Western diet barely provides the fuel we need to survive, let alone be in good health. It always surprises me when people are shocked by illness after feeding their bodies toxins for years. Most people wouldn't dream of pouring vegetable oil or liquid sugar into the gas tank of their car. Why not? Well, that's not what a car needs in order to run. Who knows, perhaps if we tried it, our car could still run for a little while. But eventually, its insides would get damaged, and it would come to a stop. It's hard to think about it in the same way, but our bodies are a vehicle designed to be fueled by what nature provides, at least mostly. We forget that we come from nature. Though we may be spiritual beings, we are also just sophisticated mammals.

You don't have to have a pristine diet or follow any specific strict diet (unless you have allergies or sensitivities or your doctor or nutritionist has advised you otherwise). Here are my go-to tips for eating:

Follow the 85/15 rule

85% of the time, eat plant-based foods (leafy green and other veggies and fruits), lean protein (beans, fish, poultry, or lean organic meat), whole grains (quinoa, oats, brown rice, millet, barley, whole wheat), and healthy fats (avocado, olive oil, fatty fish). Here's the fun part — 15% of the time, eat what you love! Enjoy pizza, ice cream, chips, a burger, chocolate, or a glass of wine. As long as it's only 15% of your diet, it will not significantly impact your health or weight.

Be open

Try different foods and new things in general. Sometimes, you might have to try something more than once to expand your palate. Cognitive flexibility is good for your body and brain.

Drink water

You need more than you think. To determine how many ounces of water you should drink per day, take your body weight in pounds and divide it in half. That is the number of ounces you should be imbibing daily. For example, if you weigh 100 pounds, you should drink 50 ounces of water a day. Coffee and alcohol don't count; in fact, add a glass of water for every cup of each you consume (they're dehydrating). Herbal teas count as water, as does fruit juice without added sugar. However, it's best to drink no more than one glass of juice per day.

Eat breakfast

This goes against the current trend of intermittent fasting, but for many people, including those with blood sugar issues, consuming a healthy breakfast is very important. A breakfast with protein, whole grains, and possibly fruit or veggie balances blood sugar, curbs hunger levels, and provides fuel for the body and brain to function optimally throughout the day.

Eat whole grains

Not all "carbs" are evil. In the anti-carb movement, we've lost nutrient-rich grains like quinoa, oats, brown rice, millet, barley, whole wheat, and more. These are all high in soluble and insoluble fiber, which helps reduce inflammation, lower cholesterol, and move things through the digestive system with more ease. What you want to avoid is heavily processed "white" carbs, like white rice and white flour, which are digested in the body as sugar.

Learn to cook

Just a few simple meals. Processed foods are convenient but filled with unrecognizable ingredients that negatively impact health. You don't have to become a chef to learn to cook simple and delicious meals. Chicken, salmon, or tofu can be easily pan-seared, baked, or broiled with simple spices. Add a cooked whole grain and side of veggies or salad, and you have a delicious, healthy meal.

Recognize whole and natural foods

Recognize what foods are processed. Don't read the nutrition label as much as the ingredient list. Do you know what those words mean? If not, don't eat it. Generally, shop the perimeter of any grocery store. The most processed items are often in the middle of the store.

Attending your physical body takes time and effort, but you are worth it. Once you develop habits that help you care for your physical self, you'll feel better and understand how the physical is connected to your other layers of being.

Balancing Your Energy

Let's look through the traditional lens of the pranamaya kosha, or the energy layer of our being. We are observing how energy moves between our physical bodies and our mental-emotional selves. Breathing practices are the traditional method to care for and balance our energy. So, while I refer you back to the section on breathwork in Part One: Mindfulness, I also want to offer other practices that overlap the physical and mental-emotional.

Forgiveness

Forgiveness can be a difficult topic because we are sometimes more comfortable holding onto resentment than letting it go. It feels righteous to remain angry at someone who wronged you or to remain angry at yourself when you feel you have erred.

To forgive is to free yourself from the hot coal of resentment burning in you. If you don't practice forgiveness, the darkness generated by resentment will create tension and perpetuate your angry feelings. Letting it go is challenging, but cutting the chains of rumination, anger, and resentment will serve both your mind and your heart.

To forgive another person for wrongdoing doesn't mean that you are condoning their behavior or choosing to make them an active part of your personal life. Forgiveness is ultimately a practice of self-love and has little to do with the person who wronged you. If it's helpful, consider this definition of forgiveness: *Forgiveness is a process of accepting and being comfortable with the fact that you cannot change your past.*

This definition of forgiveness can allow you to look at what has happened, grieve, and mindfully move forward in your life with more space in your heart. What is it like to forgive yourself or someone else? Journal about your experience with forgiveness or with holding onto resentment.

As part of a forgiveness process, I recommend the following practice daily until you start to feel energetically lighter.

Ho'oponopono Healing Meditation

A Hawaiian practice of reconciliation and forgiveness, this simple meditation is a cleansing way to process your own mistakes and, in your own heart, to forgive yourself and others and be free. Simply sit and close your eyes. Repeat the following statements silently or aloud at least three times for each scenario.

First, focus on forgiving yourself. Forgive yourself for the ways in which you have caused yourself harm through self-doubt, self-criticism, or failing to stand up for yourself. Forgive yourself for not taking care of your body or actively causing it harm. Forgive yourself for being perfectly imperfect. Say these phrases to yourself.

- I love you
- I'm sorry
- Please forgive me
- Thank you

Next, you'll repeat the same phrases for someone you've intentionally or unintentionally hurt. We all make mistakes in relationships and sometimes say the wrong thing or do the wrong thing. We unintentionally cause harm and only find out later that our words or actions hurt someone. And sometimes, we might act emotionally or reactively and cause harm. We are human, after all. Choose a person you feel you've hurt, and imagine the person is with you. Then imagine saying the phrases to them, genuinely asking for forgiveness.

Finally, repeat the phrases in a third round, imagining you're *receiving* them from someone who has caused you harm. This can be particularly helpful if you don't have a resolution in a relationship and perhaps, you're unlikely to. You can create that resolution yourself with this practice.

Afterward, you might sit in silence and just breathe, or you might cry or allow for other healthy expressions of emotion. Next, engage the 4:8 breath for a few minutes. Then get up and go outside if you can, or do something nourishing for yourself. If you haven't already created one prior to this exercise, make a list of healthy, nourishing activities you can do anytime you need a little self-love. Here's an example list. Feel free to borrow these suggestions or create your own healthy nourishment list.

Nourishment List

- Take a bath
- Take a walk
- Read inspirational poetry or quotes
- Write a poem
- Sit outside on a swing
- Write your gratitude list for the day
- Make yourself some tea and drink it slowly
- Call a good friend and catch up
- Make plans with a friend
- Listen to your favorite uplifting music

Notice how you feel after practicing both ho'oponopono and something from your nourishment list. Lifting the weight of regret, self-loathing, and resentment can help you reclaim the vital energy you need to do what you love in the world. Ultimately, you will feel better in the long run. Be patient with yourself. The process of forgiveness and healing can take time, and everyone's journey looks different.

Gratitude

I discussed a formal gratitude practice back in the mindfulness section under meditation techniques. Consider incorporating a 30-day gratitude practice at least one time, as it really can help to shift your mindset from an autopilot of negativity to one of seeking positivity in your life. Even if you don't complete the whole 30-day gratitude practice as it was outlined, you can still pause on a difficult day and balance your awareness by paying attention to the main things in your life you're thankful for.

I know it's not always easy, especially when it feels like the world is crashing down around you. Remember, gratitude isn't about pushing away difficult circumstances. It's about practicing holding space for both the pleasant and the unpleasant. Doing so will help to lift your energy up from a lower place, and even a shift of a few degrees is worth the effort.

Consider trying one of the following reminder tips to help you practice gratitude:

- Wear a beaded bracelet and deem it your gratitude bracelet; let it remind you to count your blessings.

- If you utilize Alexa or some other reminder app or AI, ask it to cue you to practice gratitude daily at a particular time.

- Make it a habit before dinner or another meal; pause and think of everything you're thankful for. Share it out loud if you eat with others. This can be a great conversation starter, too.

Letting Go

In my work as a psychotherapist, I frequently hear about the emotional pain people carry with them: memories from traumatic events and fears about the unknown future. Sometimes, people are unaware that they are carrying around residue from past events or future worries, but they just feel angry all the time or are generally unhappy. Past events and our thoughts about them, as well as future worries and assumptions, stick with us. We hold them mentally, in our emotional reactions, and in our physical bodies. Carrying all of this can deplete your energy and prevent you from living your best life.

This is why the practice of awareness and letting go is vital. I know "letting go" sounds cliche, and it is flippant when we are talking about truly heavy experiences, but it does have a place in balancing our emotional health. And besides, why would you want to hang on to your pain? Consider practicing mindful awareness of the things that scare you and give them a nod of acknowledgment by saying, *hello, emotional pain and fear, I see you.* Now, notice your feelings, allow yourself to feel them for a moment, then permit yourself to let them go. You might tell yourself, *it's okay to let this pain go or let it be.* You don't have to focus on the pain. Try visualizing your pain as a bursting balloon or dropping your troubles on a floating leaf in a stream. Watch them gently float away.

Practices like this certainly aren't "one and done," but they are a healthy way to cope with challenging thoughts or memories on a regular basis. This internal work will help you let go of the mental formations around things outside of your control again and again. It may feel more comfortable to stay stuck in your emotional pain. If you can understand that you have a choice to do something different, in time, you'll learn to notice painful memories and fears, then let them go and focus on the present moment. This is a practice of emotional freedom. You get to choose to free yourself of the baggage that you were previously carrying. You can be free. It takes mindfulness and effort, but it is worthwhile work as you care for your physical self, energetic self, and mental/emotional self.

Shinrin-Yoku

Forest bathing, or *shinrin-yoku*, is a practice coined in Japan in the 1980s that involves immersing oneself in nature for a period of time. Researched benefits include reduced tension and stress, improved mood, and an increase in creativity.[23] It makes sense: we came from nature, and in nature, we can find peace. However, we've unfortunately created a world for ourselves where we live indoors and move quickly from one indoor environment to another. We are often so disconnected from nature that we look at an app to ascertain the weather outside instead of just stepping out to experience it. Many people are unable to differentiate plants that are poisonous from those that are safe and trees that bear fruit from those that don't. And we are vastly unaware of the whole universe of insects and plant life that make up our outdoor spaces. While shinrin-yoku isn't about labeling or identifying plant and animal life around you, it's a world worth considering and learning more about.

To practice forest bathing, take a walk in the woods and find a quiet place. Either walk slowly, being mindful of sounds, sights, smells, and things you can touch, or find a place to sit and do the same. As you relax and get comfortable, you may even close your eyes (if you're sitting). Take time to be surrounded by nature. Spend at least 20 minutes or up to two hours or more outside.

Ask yourself:

- What information am I taking in with my senses?
- What is my heart telling me about this experience?
- What is my body telling me while I'm here?

Here's another way of being present in the forest:

Consider focusing on one tree. Observe it from its roots to its top. Get closer. Feel its bark. Notice the shape and texture of its leaves. Lean against it or sit with it. What might this tree tell you if it could speak to you?

If you're not used to being in nature, this will be a new experience, and your senses will have a lot to focus on. Try to relax. We come from nature. We are a part of it, and it is a part of us, no matter how much we build literal walls around ourselves. Remember, this is meant to be an immersive time in nature, so unplug from your device and from constant man-made sound. In fact, leave your phone at home, in your car, or at least turn it off while you're in the forest. Journal or contemplate your experience with shinrin-yoku. Go outside every day if you can, or at least once a week if you live in a city.

Socialization vs. Time Alone

In Part Two: Discovery and perhaps earlier in your life, you learned that you tended towards being either an introvert, who is primarily refueled by time alone, or an extrovert, who is primarily refueled by socialization. This is important information to remember when you feel burned out or overwhelmed. However, introverts shouldn't necessarily be hermits, and even extroverts need alone time sometimes. Consider paying close attention to where you are currently on this spectrum of socialization vs. alone time and how it relates to your innate tendencies of introversion or extroversion. You might consider stepping outside your comfort zone to create balance and reap the benefits of both seemingly opposite traits.

Human beings are social creatures, inherently. In fact, we are pack or herd animals. Primitive nomadic people traveled in groups where everyone had a specific role in keeping everyone alive and well. If you, as an individual, wandered away from the group or struck out on your own, you were likely to either be killed by a predator or starve to death. While that isn't quite the case anymore, it is still important to consider that the internal need for belonging is alive in all of us as a core human need.

Belonging is the feeling of being seen, accepted, loved, and supported just as you are. This is, in part, why groups around certain traits, interests, or beliefs are formed in our culture: sports, religion, politics, sexual orientation, gender, or pop culture interests fulfill the need to belong. Research indicates that belonging can create a greater overall sense of happiness and well-being and a reduction in anxiety, depression, and feelings of loneliness or hopelessness. Socialization, in general, can lighten your mood, lower your risk of dementia, promote a sense of safety and security, and improve overall brain health.[24]

One problem in our modern world post-COVID-19 is that we are working remotely more, connecting online more, and engaging in fewer face-to-face interactions. And because we lose non-verbal communication nuances when interacting via text, email, social media, or virtual reality settings (nonverbal usually makes up 70% to 90% of our communication), we don't get the same feelings of belonging and connection. In fact, we may be lonelier, more anxious, and more depressed than ever. "Social" media is at our fingertips, but it doesn't have the same impact as the face-to-face connection our ancestors had when we lived in and traveled in groups. There will be more of this in Part Four: Connection.

I want to encourage you to consider your "socialization health" and how you might enhance it. Try joining a yoga class, gym, book club, dance class, hiking group, or church. Or connect with those already in your life by hosting a game night, costume party, potluck, picnic, or holiday event. Think of a cause you're passionate about and research a local chapter that meets to chat or volunteer. And, for you extroverts out there, don't overdo it.

This leads us to discuss the importance of having alone time. If you're an introvert, you might already be enjoying your solo activities, but perhaps you could consider whether they are inherently mindful or distracting and create more balance. For some extroverts, alone time can be downright terrifying. However, spending time alone offers us a wonderful opportunity to self-reflect and practice self-discovery. By spending time alone, you get to know yourself through understanding and accepting your history, strengths, and growth edges. Then you can create a path toward mental, emotional, physical, and spiritual wellness and happiness.

Ask yourself what happens when you are alone. Do you immediately want to fill the space with noise, such as music, television, the news, or a podcast? There's nothing wrong with any of those things in moderation. They can be beneficial in many ways. But if you can't stand to be silent with yourself, you might get curious and ask yourself, *why?* What is so uncomfortable inside that you want to drown it out? Is it a memory? Your inner voice? A particular fear?

Try to take some time in silence to just sit still for about five minutes. What's happening in your body? Make a note of it or even write it in your journal. Notice what thoughts and emotions arise. Write them down or at least name them. Make this a regular practice. Have no expectations for yourself. You are just seeing what happens when you are alone. In time, you can expand and complete practices in this book or another fulfilling activity you enjoy. Of course, alone time doesn't have to be in silent reflection only. Many people enjoy hiking, vacationing, reading, or pursuing a creative endeavor in solitude. I invite you to notice how you feel when you are alone in reflection and when you're alone involved in an activity. Figure out how much alone time you want and need compared to socialization. And make sure you're getting both, whether you're an introvert or extrovert.

Sleep

Getting good quality sleep seems to be one of the biggest struggles we have in our culture right now. When I ask the people I work with about their sleep habits and quality of sleep, I frequently hear that they can't fall asleep, aren't getting enough sleep, or are sleeping "enough" but are still exhausted.

Lack of sleep can wreak havoc on the mind, body, and emotions. At a minimum, lack of sleep causes irritability, anxiousness, and problems with attention. At worst, chronic sleep deprivation can create inflammation in the body and increase the risk of high blood pressure, heart disease, stroke, obesity, and depression.[25]

Treating your sleep struggles can be tricky because the underlying causes vary. The first step is to look at your sleep hygiene, which is your routine right before bedtime. Here are my tips for good sleep hygiene. You probably can't commit to following all of these recommendations every night, but consider trying several to see if anything improves for you:

- Do a "mind dump" before bed: In a journal or notebook, write everything that pops into your mind at bedtime (tomorrow's to-do list, last-minute reminders, reflections about today).

- Go to sleep and wake up at roughly the same time every day (even on the weekends).

- Eliminate all screens (including your phone) one hour before bed.

- Don't watch the news in the late evening, especially if you're bothered by it.

- Read something pleasant before bed.

- Listen to soft music.

- Keep the lights dim in the evening.

- Move more slowly, with intention, around your house in the evening.

- Get enough exercise during the day.

- Don't drink alcohol within two hours of bedtime, and don't drink excessively. Alcohol might make you feel sleepy, but it will disrupt the quality of your sleep.

- If you wake up to use the bathroom in the middle of the night, limit fluids altogether four hours before bed (but stay hydrated the rest of the day).

- Take a warm bath or shower about 30 minutes before bedtime.

- Consider listening to a guided meditation or sleep relaxation, like something on Insight Timer or another app.

- Keep your bedroom cool, but have blankets available to keep yourself warm.

- Use calming essential oils like lavender, either in a diffuser or rub some on your wrists or elsewhere.

- Check with your doctor to see if you can use something natural like melatonin or valerian as an occasional supplement.

- If practicing these tips doesn't help, check with your doctor. You might need blood work or other testing to see if you have an underlying condition causing your insomnia.

Consider what might be zapping your energy and how you can cultivate greater balance through forgiveness, gratitude, socialization, solitude, and rest. Remember, our energy impacts our minds and our bodies, for better or worse.

Supporting Your Mental and Emotional Wellness

Most of us grapple from time to time with issues affecting our mental and emotional selves and require some kind of support. If there was a silver lining to the COVID-19 pandemic, it is that it brought mental health to the forefront of everyone's awareness. What was an already growing upward trend of anxiety, depression, and suicide rates increased at an alarming pace. In part, this may have been due to the state of isolation. As we discussed in Balancing your Energy, socialization is an essential part of being human. But there are likely many other factors at play as well. As we plow full steam ahead with technologies like artificial intelligence (AI) that have the potential to make our lives easier and more convenient in some ways, we need to hold space for and support mental and emotional wellness because those same advances could potentially rob us of our humanity.

There is nothing that an app or AI can tell you about yourself that will fix the feeling of unrest or distress inside. As individuals and as a culture, we must turn to the low-tech practice of simple awareness. Although challenging, we need to cultivate awareness of our bodies, energy, and mental/emotional state without depending on an app, a smartwatch, or some external AI diagnostic to tell us what's happening inside. Without our inner awareness, we can't live life to the fullest.

Without the ability to pay attention, we can't truly appreciate the wonderful elements of human life. AI can't replace the heartfelt and fulfilling experience of seeing the sunrise over a mountain you hiked or the face of someone you love deeply after being separated. It can't replace the sensation of a cool breeze on a sunny day or a comforting touch. It can't replace the luscious taste of your favorite food, the sounds of birds chirping or a moving piece of music, the aroma of your grandmother's banana bread, or the smell of an alpine meadow after a rain. Nor can it duplicate the words of a poet that pull at your heartstrings or the connection you feel when you learn someone else has experienced what you have. And how could it ever be a viable substitute for the feeling of accomplishment when you complete a challenging task?

There are AI virtual reality simulations that might create similar experiences, but living fully means living in reality. Part of the challenge in cultivating mental and emotional wellness is that we suffer so much because we are not in the reality of the present moment. Rather, we dwell in a fictitious reality in our minds. Events and circumstances happen to us, and we overlay their meaning with stories in our minds. These stories can be positive and involve gratitude and pleasure. But they are often about how we think others are judging us or rejecting us, or we are rejecting and judging others, or we spiral about how we aren't good enough and reinforce that story with the fear-related thoughts we have in our heads. I've touched on this in various sections of the book and simply wish to reinforce it here. We must cultivate awareness and support for our inner mental and emotional space. We must be able to untangle ourselves and see it clearly, learn to accept it for what it is, and then practice self-control with our thoughts and emotions, something an app cannot do for us.

Meditation

Because meditation is a practice that helps focus the mind and regulate emotions, it is the most highly recommended action you can take in caring for your mental and emotional self. As discussed in Part One: Mindfulness, there are many techniques you can try. Choose a technique or two you enjoy or one that seems to help you, and practice those regularly. Practice every day if you can, even if only for just five or ten minutes. This is brain training and will help you learn to see your thoughts instead of being enmeshed with them. You will learn that you can take control of your mind. You don't have to follow a line of thought simply because it popped into your head. You can choose to let it go and try to see objective reality as much as possible. You might plant a positive thought to help to calm your emotions. Meditation techniques aid in this training, like a rehearsal for life. When you are living day to day, you can learn to apply what you discover on your cushion (or chair) to life's ever-changing circumstances. You will feel more focused mentally and more calm emotionally.

Journaling

The idea of journaling might make you cringe, or it might be something you enjoy; many seem to have polar opposite opinions about it. However, writing out your thoughts and feelings is a great way to process them because you see them on paper. You can understand yourself with a bit more clarity and objectivity. Sometimes, venting on paper about something you are going through feels good. You may even choose to tear up the paper or burn it (in a safe, contained way) when you are done, as a symbolic gesture of letting go. If you don't want to write words in your journal, you can draw or doodle based on how you feel and what's going on in your mind.

If you'd like specific journal prompts to get you started, here are a few to consider. You don't have to answer all of them; just select the ones that speak to you.

- Where or when have you felt the most connected to something greater, like a higher power or even your best self? What did this look like? Journal about all the details and the feelings of this experience.

- What is the difference between "grasping" and "opening or allowing"? What might this idea look like in reality? How can you relate this to your own life?

- Define grace (your definition). What role does grace play in your life? What can it help you do? Consider these words and write what they mean to you: Grace, Forgiveness, Letting Go, Practice, Compassion.

- Discuss your own balance between strength and softness, sthira sukha, in your life. Where do you need more of one or the other? What does this mean to you?

- What do you wish people understood about you?

Haiku

Igniting a creative spark can help you feel, understand, and process your emotions differently, so please consider trying it by writing a haiku. A haiku is a traditional Japanese poetry style that often focuses on images from nature, and it follows a specific format. A haiku is three lines. The first line contains five syllables, the second seven syllables, and the third five syllables. Seventeen syllables in total. Then, pick a title for it. Consider how you feel and try to relate it to something in nature. Let's get started. Here are two examples I've written. Can you guess the feelings I was processing?

Young at Heart

With lightness and play
Excited for each new turn
Child-like wonder glows.

Procrastination

The vile unknown thief
Willingly robbed my dear time
Sadly, it was me.

You could also consider writing prose style of poetry (unstructured) if it suits you better. I'm offering you many tools and options to practice care, so if this one doesn't speak to you, that's okay.

Restorative Yoga

Restorative yoga is a specific practice that requires various props: blankets, pillows or bolsters, and possibly yoga blocks, straps, and an eye pillow. In this practice, you set yourself up in relaxing postures where all the props completely support your body. You stay for a minimum of ten minutes in each pose. If you can get the body to relax deeply, your mind will eventually follow. The entry point is opposite to meditation, where we work with the mind to relax the mind and body. Restorative yoga — especially the more you practice it — trains your body and mind to melt into the present moment in comfort. Many people find this practice to be an exceptionally relaxing experience.

If you find a class in your area, ask questions about what the class is like because there are many impostor restorative yoga classes. Some will call gentle movement classes or yin yoga classes "restorative." But in true restorative yoga, you might only change positions three times in an hour-long class. You are resting, napping, and relaxing the rest of the time. It's a different kind of yoga practice. I highly recommend the book *Relax and Renew: Restful Yoga for Stressful Times* by Judith Hanson Lasater. Judith trained me, and she is indeed the queen of guiding this practice. Judith recommends doing one restorative posture per day (for 15 minutes), one hour of restorative postures once per week, and for one week per year, an hour of restorative postures each day. I did this for years when my children were young; I even taught my younger child to practice with me. It helped me manage my stress and stay calm in all sorts of precarious situations. Read a book on restorative yoga, watch a video, or find a class in your area. Know that in your first experience, you might simply learn how busy your mind is and how tense your body is. That's okay. Remember that awareness is always the first step. The more you practice it, the more you will learn how to relax.

Cognitive Flexibility

I've mentioned the importance of perspective multiple times. Being open to new ideas and experiences and willing to try to see things from another perspective is all part of cognitive flexibility. If you practice this, you'll be able to adapt to circumstances with greater ease and gain insight into yourself, others, and the situation at hand.

How do you practice cognitive flexibility? It's a matter of exercising your "muscles" of perception during practices like meditation. It's about being mindful in a moment and realizing when you are stuck in "things being a certain way." It comes down to awareness. When even a small part of you can see or name what's happening in your mind, you immediately gain control and can choose what happens next. Remember to be playful with yourself if you're able to. I try to say something inside like, *huh, look at that. I'm doing "that thing" again.* That thing is the autopilot habit, the stuck, narrow view. Be curious and creative. Consider taking the opposite view for just a moment or just think the opposite view. This can help you see that there are options. Life is usually not black or white, but many illustrious shades of gray. We need to realize that we are not at the mercy of the thoughts in our minds. We are capable of shifting our thoughts, our opinions, our beliefs. We are not at the mercy of our mind's first rambling thought.

There's an old story of a man riding very fast on a horse. As he rides by his friend, who is standing on the side of the road, the friend calls out, "Where are you going?" The man looks toward his friend and shouts, "I don't know, ask the horse!"

Don't let your wild horse (your mind) drag you around. Practice taking the reins. You can learn to notice and redirect your line of thinking. It's not easy, but you can learn how. One step at a time.

Attitude Adjustment: From Resistance to Acceptance

Attitude adjustment goes along with cognitive flexibility. Sometimes, we all need an attitude adjustment when we can get stuck in a certain way of being in a pattern of reactivity. Hopefully, you have at least one good friend, or perhaps your spouse, who can gently or humorously point out when you're stuck and need to shift. Even though I've practiced all the things in these pages, I was recently stuck, while moving through a particularly tough life transition. I arranged to meet some dear friends for dinner, and they did a great job of first empathizing with me and then guiding me toward a perspective shift of gratitude.

I realized that I had been stuck in a state of resistance. I didn't want this transition to occur. I wanted to cling to the past. But there was nothing I could do to change it or stop it. It was happening whether I liked it or not. But by resisting reality, I was unconsciously creating a lot of tension in my body and mind, and upset in my emotions. My eyes opened when my friends gently helped me see that I was stuck in the negatives about the transition. Their support made it easier for me to give myself the attitude adjustment I needed.

There's a saying, "What you resist persists. What you accept transforms you." Sometimes, we have to accept difficult realities in life that we really don't want: the loss of someone we love, a divorce, the loss of a job, children growing up and moving away, our bodies changing as we age. These things happen, and fighting against the reality of them makes it harder to move through the transition into a new life. Instead, the attitude adjustment might just be saying to yourself inside, *Yep. This is happening. Yep. I don't like it. But it's happening.* It's a reality statement. When you can sit with reality and get comfortable, then you can consider the adjustment, *What can I be thankful for? Can I acknowledge the experience before this? Can I appreciate my good health, love, friendship, and support?* Find the sweet in the bittersweet elements of life. It's all too easy to stay with the bitter.

Self-Compassion

We also need to be gentle with ourselves inside. Too often, we beat ourselves up in our minds and with our moods. There's a heartbreaking mental health phenomenon in which people practice self-harm as a way of managing difficult moments and thoughts. Some of these people literally cut themselves to the point of bleeding, and this cutting behavior somehow feels right to the person in distress. While this kind of cutting is a rare practice, all of us end up cutting ourselves on the inside, where no one can see. We cut ourselves with the terrible things we say to ourselves, with ridiculously high expectations, and never taking a moment to applaud ourselves for our successes.

Notice what's going on in your mind and in your heart. Be as gentle with yourself as you would be with a very young child or an adorable puppy. This doesn't mean that you enable yourself to stay stuck. This doesn't mean you don't accept responsibility for your mistakes or complain to everyone you know about your struggles. This doesn't mean you lie in bed day after day when you're depressed and say that you are practicing self-compassion. That's enabling. We need to check ourselves and find a balance between effort and ease. Hard work and rest. Sthira and sukha. Drive and gentleness. Too much of one or the other isn't helpful on the path of growth. Take some time each week to reflect and see where you are. Work toward overall balance, knowing that it's normal for the scales to tip one way or the other from day to day.

Therapy

On this path toward self-compassion, you might consider talking to a therapist. It can be helpful to share what's going on in your life and inside your mind and heart. And while venting about your struggles can be helpful, remember that just like everything else, we need to find balance here as well. In other words, talk about your struggles, but not too much. Suppose you tell everyone about your bad day or difficult circumstances. In that case, you are creating a cycle of living in that difficulty because you're experiencing it repeatedly each time you tell the story. This fuels the negative feelings that go along with the unpleasant circumstances. You'll either feel worse or self-righteous in your self-pity, which is different from self-compassion. A good therapist will help you in this process. Remember to focus on everything in your life, not just what's difficult. Acknowledge the good, too. Learn to see it and hold space for it all.

Getting Things Done

Getting Things Done by David Allen discusses how to be productive. I'm not talking about being a workaholic but engaging in healthy productivity. Knowing how to manage your time and complete tasks efficiently means you don't have to work all the time. This topic is under the mental and emotional care section because most of us get stressed when we can't complete the projects and tasks on our physical or mental to-do list. Many people I counsel are overwhelmed, in part because they've never learned how to be productive.

I can't do this whole topic justice here, but these are my highlights on how to be more organized and effective at getting things done:

Know the difference between a task and a project

A task is one step of a project. Sometimes, a task might just take a few minutes, or it could take a few hours. A project is a series of many tasks. Let me give you an example.

If you put "paint the kitchen" on your to-do list but never seem to get it done, the reason is that it's a project and shouldn't be on your "to-do" list. The "paint the kitchen" project contains the following tasks:

1. Go to the store and get paint color chips/cards.
2. Bring the color chips home and hold them up against your walls or other things that need to match or contrast in color.
3. Decide on the color.
4. Figure out how much paint you'll need to buy.
5. Research brands and types of paint.
6. Decide on the type of paint.
7. Go back to the paint store and purchase the paint and supplies.
8. Bring it home and schedule an afternoon for painting.
9. Tape off the trim and cabinets, then lay drop cloths.
10. Get the supplies ready and stage them in the kitchen.
11. Paint the kitchen.
12. Clean up your supplies and paint tape.

Each of those tasks belongs on a to-do list at some point, possibly not all in one day. Look at your to-do list and determine if you have listed tasks or multi-step projects. If you can break down any project into bite-sized pieces, you'll get more done and feel more productive and successful. In short, know the difference between a task and a project.

Time Management

No one is perfect at managing their time, and we are surrounded by potential distractions every day. Activities like social media scrolling, texting, watching cat videos or TikTok, or even small tasks like deciding to reorganize or clean can waste time that could be used to accomplish something necessary or important on your list. A client of mine referred to this as revenge procrastination. It often happens when we are overwhelmed, and it feels like we don't have enough time to "get it all done," so we self-sabotage and don't even try. We somehow feel justified in our revenge procrastination, but simultaneously, it perpetuates the cycle of being overwhelmed and staying stuck behind the long to-do list.

Here are a few ideas to consider when thinking about your relationship with time:

Time feels like it speeds up, and you don't have enough when you:

- take in more information than you can process.
- set unrealistic deadlines for yourself.
- fill your calendar with activities and appointments back-to-back.

Time will feel slower, and you realize you have enough when you

- give yourself one-minute breaks every hour to close your eyes and breathe slowly.
- remove three non-essential tasks or events from your to-do list without doing them. Don't fill this space.
- remove social media apps from your phone or use an app that helps you dramatically limit their use.

There are great books to help you get organized and manage your time more effectively. I've offered you just a few of my tips to get you started on being productive so you have time to do the things that are important to you.

Perspective

In some ways, this entire book is about perspective or ways of seeing things differently. In this section, I have one final note and a couple of stories left to share about perspective and caring for your mental and emotional health. This is important because you create your own mental heaven or hell according to how you perceive your circumstances. Often, what we think we experience is tied to an ironclad perspective, which may or may not have anything to do with reality.

In her book *Living Your Yoga*, Judith Hansen Lasater tells an old story of a farmer experiencing stress and overwhelm. The story goes something like this: A farmer goes to the local rabbi for help and says, "Rabbi, I don't know what to do. My life is so chaotic. At home, I live with my wife, mother-in-law, four children, six chickens, two cows, three sheep, and two cats. I can't take it anymore!" The rabbi says that he can help. He instructs the man to buy a goat. The farmer thanks the rabbi and does as he suggests. He returns a week later, "Rabbi, things are even more chaotic than before! Now, I live with my wife, mother-in-law, four children, six chickens, two cows, three sheep, two cats, and a goat! There's an increase in the chaos!" Again, the rabbi says he can help. He instructs the man to sell the goat. The farmer respectfully thanks the rabbi and does as he suggests. The next week, he returns to the rabbi with a smile, "Rabbi, that worked! Things are wonderful at home. Now, all I have are my wife, mother-in-law, four children, six chickens, two cows, three sheep, and two cats. Things are positively peaceful without that goat!"[26] What once seemed like hell now seems like heaven!

Did anything change for the farmer? Or was he able to experience a reduction in his stress level simply because he gained a new, embodied perspective?

An old philosophical puzzle one of my teachers posed also speaks about perspective: if you are a tiger in a cage, what keeps you inside?

Most might answer quickly and simply that it's the bars; the cage keeps the tiger inside. However, this is not true at all. It's not the bars that keep the tiger confined. It's the space between the bars. The tiger could walk right through if there was more space between the bars. So, are our thoughts trapping us? Or is it the lack of space between them? We might see another viewpoint or widen the space between our bars by slowing down. Then we can learn to shift from what seems simple at first, but after a pause, can open up a whole different perspective.

You might sometimes feel stuck in your own cage, stuck because the spaces between the bars are too narrow; there's simply too much noise in your mind. But the wonderful truth is that you can widen those spaces and learn how to escape your mind's cage. The whole world of perspective is available when you are mindful, aware, and present, no matter your circumstances. Mindfulness practices are the key to unlocking your cage, the key to enabling this shift in perspective. By becoming familiar with and befriending the content of your mind, you can learn to let go and center yourself. Then, the door to broader perspectives opens.

There are many tools that help support mental and emotional wellness: therapy, journaling, restorative yoga, learning how to be balanced in your productivity, and of course, cognitive flexibility and perspective shifting. Consider what works for you and commit to its regular practice.

Cultivating Your Wisdom

What is wisdom, anyway? According to the koshas, wisdom is that experience of innate, deep knowing. Some might refer to it as instinct; others would call it intuition. Some would say it's a conglomeration of acquired and applied knowledge. What it isn't is book smarts or what we might think of as traditional intelligence. You don't read your way to wisdom; it doesn't matter how many credentials you have after your name. It's with you, or you don't yet know how to access it.

There are three types of wisdom: inherited, applied, and spiritual.

Inherited Wisdom

Wisdom can, in part, be inherited from the generations before us. The study of epigenetics shows that we have DNA markers that are either prone to being switched on or off, as a result of what previous generations have experienced, as well as from environmental factors. Often, epigenetics is discussed in psychology around trauma responses we might inherit from our parents and grandparents. However, positive expressions can be inherited too. In family systems, a few generations ago, grandfathers, fathers, and sons all worked in the same industry. While some of this might have been familial expectation and social structure, there's also a degree of aptitude that's passed on. For instance, if your ancestors were farmers, engineers, or chefs for generations, an epigenetic switch might be turned on in you that gives you a leg up on understanding such things. In my case, I genetically come from several generations of engineers. I myself was never trained as one nor raised by one. However, I have this innate curiosity and sometimes an ability to fix or build things using logic I can't explain but I understand. This differs from learned knowledge. Inherited wisdom offers a propensity for certain kinds of knowledge or skills. Studying what you already have a propensity towards will certainly increase knowledge and skill while cultivating applied wisdom. In a simpler sense, think of how quickly and easily pre-teens can navigate new technology. This wisdom may also be environmental, as they've grown up with it. Epigenetic science doesn't argue nature vs. nurture; it confirms that it's a bit of both. So, in terms of understanding life around us, we all come equipped with some degree of what we will call "inherited wisdom."

Applied Wisdom

A second type of wisdom, called applied wisdom, is more about what we live and breathe combined with what we study. In other words, our embodied experience cultivates wisdom. Malcolm Gladwell discusses some of this in his book *Blink: The Power of Thinking Without Thinking*. Applied wisdom is how experts in certain fields can make quick, accurate observations and decisions. For example, art experts can discern a fake painting from an original in a "blink"; bodyworkers can tell where you hold tension or have an injury just by looking at your posture; and mechanics can ascertain what's wrong with an engine based on a "hunch" by briefly looking at or listening to it. Examples like these could go on and on. These types of quick, accurate assessments are not the same as critical thinking or analysis, and they certainly do not involve overthinking. Rather, this kind of wisdom occurs through instinct bolstered by training, personal experience, embodiment, and maybe some inherited wisdom.

We can't gain wisdom simply by reading a few books on a topic, but if we apply what we learn and gain our own knowledge through experience, again and again…punah punah…we can have something special. We can have wisdom about our little corner of the world. And that wisdom can be accessed and utilized instantly if we get out of our own way and don't get stuck in overthinking. Some might refer to this as mental or emotional wisdom, which accompanies high emotional intelligence.

Spiritual or Psychic Wisdom

The third possible type of wisdom is esoteric, originating from an unknown source, perhaps spiritual, divine, or related to the universal laws of connection. This is the kind of wisdom demonstrated in circumstances we can't explain. Some might call it instinct or intuition. Perhaps you have a gut feeling that someone you love is in danger, and later, you find out you were right. Or the moment before the phone rings, you think of the person who ends up calling you. Some who embody this type of wisdom can sense things before they happen, and their sense is accurate much of the time. We might call these people mystics, psychics, or intuitives. We all have varying capabilities with this kind of wisdom; we just have to learn to get out of our own way to access it. Spiritual wisdom is like the fourth innermost doll in a Russian nesting doll in which each larger doll represents one of the koshas. We have to learn to balance (or open) the first three kosha layers, the physical, energetic, and mental emotional, before we can truly access the depth of the wisdom that's inside. Ideally, as we move forward on our journey, we are realizing and cultivating all three: inherited, applied, and spiritual wisdom. Let's discuss how you might care for your wisdom.

Cultivate Clear Vision

Part of accessing your wisdom is seeing reality as clearly as you can, which means as objectively as you can. Objectivity requires the ability to step outside of your own opinion, emotions, and ego-centric view. Of course, this is not easy and requires practice, patience, and perspective; words we return to again and again. But how do you cultivate this type of wisdom? In addition to understanding what wisdom is and how to access it, I suggest you sit with and practice the following wisdom-oriented concepts.

Be Humble & Be Open

Getting to know yourself and engaging in mindfulness practices will help you build your ability to own your shortcomings without overly criticizing yourself. This mindful self-awareness can cultivate your ability to see reality more clearly so that you can take charge of what you have control over (yourself) and let go of what you can't (other people's actions). That's wisdom in action.

Sometimes, seeing clearly is more challenging than we realize, and it's not until we are struck with a cosmic two-by-four to the head that we learn how blind we are. I'm reminded of a humorous little story of unknown origin that illustrates this point perfectly.

A man was stuck on his rooftop in a flood. He was praying to God for help. After a while, someone came by in a rowboat and shouted, "I can save you; climb in my boat."

The stranded man on his roof said, "No, thank you. God will save me."

A little while later, a man in a motorboat came by, "Jump in, sir; you can ride in my boat to safety."

The man on his roof said, "No, God will save me."

Soon, a helicopter flew low toward the stranded man, and a man shouted, "I can throw you a rope and lift you to safety."

The man on his roof shook his head no, "God will save me, I have faith," and waved the helicopter away.

Finally, the water rose, and the man on his roof drowned. When he arrived in heaven, he asked God, "I prayed and prayed. I had so much faith. Why didn't you save me?"

God replied, "I sent you a rowboat, a motorboat, and a helicopter. What more did you expect?"

While this story is a joke, the funny part is that we all have done this, although perhaps not to this extreme. We often have very specific expectations of how things should turn out. Sometimes, we are so attached to this ideal that we are blind to real, honest opportunities that come our way. Being humble and open is about recognizing that our own insight is often limited. Considering other perspectives helps us to see more clearly and receive the good fortune and blessings the universe has to offer.

One way of employing such openness is considering the philosophy "all things happen for a reason" and accepting that you might not see all the pieces of the puzzle. Remember that the world doesn't revolve around you. I'm not being flippant; it's a serious point to remember and a challenging one because we are in our own heads and bodies 24/7. "All things happen for a reason" means that events unfold as intricate pieces of a complex puzzle. Perhaps something negative happens to you because you're merely a piece in someone else's puzzle. In other words, remember to step outside your ego-centric view.

If you don't believe that "all things happen for a reason," then you can at least set out to learn something from every negative experience. It is possible to be humble, helpful, and value yourself as a human being. This is how you cultivate wisdom. Don't sweat the small stuff, and practice stepping back to see the bigger picture.

Don't Believe Everything You Think

Most of us identify way too much with our thoughts. Of course we do; they're coming from us, right? Wisdom asks us to remember that our thoughts aren't always facts; they are a conglomeration of past events and experiences that create a lens through which we view current events and experiences. In other words, you might be reliving your traumatic, hurtful memories and using them to create a narrative that may be self-righteous, self-deprecating, or a little of both. Layered on top of that is the fear of making a mistake, being wrong, or not being liked. Additionally, there are expectations for the future, both short and long-term. Plus, the voices of those who have praised or insulted you still echo inside your mind. Familial and relational patterns also play into thought processes. Finally, a multitude of media influences how you think, whether you like it or not. Are you seeing a pattern here? There's a lot of noise in your head. And when you are formulating your thoughts and making decisions, all these things come into play, whether you realize it or not.

This is, once again, why mindfulness is essential. If you can pay attention to your thoughts and be curious about them without getting roped into the narrative, you will learn to see all of the woven threads more clearly. You will be able to discern the facts from the turmoil of unsubstantiated thoughts inside your head. And when you need to, you'll be able to let them go, making it possible to step back and see another perspective or explore other avenues of thinking and being instead of your autopilot approach. This is wisdom in action. We can't blindly believe everything we think.

Know the Difference between Knowledge, Skill, and Embodiment

Knowledge is what you learn in school and by reading books. It is valuable, and it gives you a wealth of information. If you're good at remembering what you learn, even better. Facts are important in a world where everyone is trying to influence you one way or another. Knowledge broadens your perspective and can help you discern what's best in various circumstances. Keep gaining knowledge, but don't stop there.

Skill is the practice of what you know to be the correct or right way of doing something. It involves putting your knowledge to good use again and again until you become adept at implementing something you can perform consistently. Skill can be improved with practice and experience.

Embodiment is living and breathing what you know to be truth. This is when you've advanced your knowledge and skill so much that you are living mind, body, and spirit in alignment with something that has become part of you. An example is when you see someone like Yo-Yo Ma playing the cello. There's such an ease. It's as if the music flows from some deep place within him. When you see champion dancers, athletes, and artists, you'll notice this quality of embodiment. They are fully connected to themselves and their craft. Embodiment is a place where you are living your applied and spiritual (and possibly inherited) wisdom all at once.

It's important to differentiate between knowledge, skill, and embodiment and to be honest with yourself about where you are and where you'd like to be. I know plenty of people who read about mindfulness and think they're impacted by it. Then they hit traffic and emotionally blow up.

Knowledge alone is not wisdom; it is just a piece of the puzzle. We must learn to practice and fully embody the things we want to embrace in our lives. Living in wisdom means stepping forward and using knowledge and skill throughout everything you experience, punah punah. We will make mistakes. We will fall down. This is an essential part of our growth and how we cultivate wisdom. If we never made mistakes, we'd not have such wonderful opportunities to learn, develop new skills, and eventually make them a part of who we are and how we move through the world. So, whether you're reading about a new art technique, business strategy, or personal improvement practice, if it makes sense to you, take the time and effort to integrate it into your routine and form a new habit, little by little, so you will eventually embody it as your own wisdom.

Get Out of Your Primitive Brain

It is important to understand how the different regions of our brains work and what happens when we are under stress.

Stress engages our sympathetic nervous system, or the "fight, flight, or freeze" reaction. This part of your autonomic nervous system is there to respond to life-or-death emergencies. I refer to it as the emergency response system. It's meant to be engaged when you are in acute stress, like if you encounter a bear in the woods. In this state, your body produces stress hormones that increase your heart rate and blood pressure, tense your muscles, and provide a surge of energy so that you can "fight" the bear, "flee" from the bear, or "freeze" and hope the bear doesn't see you. In our modern culture, we, unfortunately, have this stress reaction not because we are necessarily under threat of being eaten by a wild animal but because our bodies *perceive* our circumstances as life-threatening. Stuck in traffic? Your heart beats out of your chest, blood pressure increases, tension creeps into your shoulders, and anxiety causes panic. You might feel this way in a host of circumstances, such as when your to-do list is long, when you have to speak to a large group, or when a situation doesn't unfold as expected. All this stress accumulates, becoming a chronic stress response that affects your brain.

When under chronic stress, your hippocampus, where learning and memory occur, begins to lose gray matter and neural connectivity. Your prefrontal cortex (the executive functioning region of your brain where logic, reason, and impulse control take place) starts to shrink, and there's less activity there, as well. And finally, the primitive amygdala region (what I call the "freak out" center, which triggers the sympathetic nervous system) gets bigger and more robust. What this all means is that your brain, when under chronic stress, interprets more of your circumstances as "life or death emergencies" because that strong amygdala is in charge and refuses to allow traffic (stimuli) to go to the logic and reason center (prefrontal cortex). In other words, the more stressed you are, the more stressed you continually feel and get stuck reacting to everything as if you were being attacked.

So, how can you have the space to choose wisdom if you are stuck on a stress hamster wheel? I've already given you the answer. By pausing. Taking deep breaths. Learning to manage stress through regular mindfulness and meditation practices, positive thinking exercises, and self-care of various kinds. Research has shown that mindfulness practices can help strengthen neural connections and increase gray matter in stress-diminished areas of the prefrontal cortex and hippocampus.[27] And regular mindfulness helps to shrink that pesky amygdala so that you don't perceive everything that comes your way as a danger. The more you practice, the more you're training your brain to be open to logic and broader views. In other words, the more you practice, the more you are able to get out of your primitive brain.

Wisdom Practices

Read Wisdom Texts

I mentioned wisdom texts in the Finding Meaning section of Part Two: Discovery. Which one speaks to you? Which do you want to read? These days, many people I speak with say they aren't readers. I get it. In our fast-paced world, it's hard to slow down and be patient enough to allow words on a page to slowly fill you with knowledge and new perspectives. It's hard to make time and do nothing but sit and read. While I want to encourage you to try to read wisdom texts you're interested in, there are many ways to get started digesting this sort of material.

I started by finding and collecting inspiring quotes from the Bible, the Yoga Sutras, the Bhagavad Gita, the Dhammapada, and others. Passages from these books and the teachers who referred to them inspired me and helped to expand my perspective. In time, I gained the patience and curiosity to want to read the actual texts on my own, to see what insight I could garner from those ancient pages.

Another option for accessing wisdom texts is audiobooks, audio training, or textual commentary. This is a great way to introduce yourself to the material, particularly if you can find an interesting and engaging narrator.

You don't have to read wisdom texts day in and day out, but I believe it's an important part of your growth in terms of getting outside of your everyday life and seeing a higher perspective. Millions of people return to these sorts of texts for a reason. Explore and be open to reading more than one. Notice the connections.

Set Intentions to Live By

> *Happiness is when what you think, what you say, and what you do are all in alignment.* ~Mahatma Gandhi

Gandhi's words speak to authenticity, which I believe can be cultivated in part through the practice of setting an intention, repeating that intention, and trying to live by that intention. Doing so lets you focus your thoughts, energy, and behavior in a higher direction. It reminds you of your chosen path and can help you take responsibility for your actions and life. The practice of repeating an intention word or phrase can help shift your mental focus from one of suffering to one alight with conscious, flexible perception. This shift can help you overcome your hurdles with greater resilience.

When you set your intention, don't be wordy or complex. You aren't setting a goal. It's an attitude you are working to embody, day by day, moment to moment. Consider choosing a word or phrase that resonates with you. An intention is growth-oriented, not a strength you already have, so pick words or qualities you don't come by naturally. Don't worry if working with your phrase feels challenging; you'll grow into it over time. Additionally, these words might change from week to week, month to month, or yearly. Or perhaps you will keep the same intention, as I have, across your lifespan. Here's a possible list of intention words:

Patience
Peace
Ease
Strength
Focus
Humor
Acceptance
Softness
Love
Connection
Surrender
Be gentle
Be flexible
Slow down
I am open
I can
I know
I trust

Consider adding to this list, then asking yourself what you need. What quality would help you move through difficult times? The word patience has helped me repeatedly when I've faced challenges in life. It's a guiding principle I will forever work with and practice. Don't expect yourself to implement your intention word with perfection. It's only a guide for getting you back on your path again and again. Punah punah.

The World as a Mirror

> *People get into a heavy-duty sin and guilt trip, feeling that if things are going wrong, that means that they did something bad and they are being punished. That's not the idea at all. The idea of karma is that you continually get the teachings that you need to open your heart. To the degree that you didn't understand in the past how to stop protecting your soft spot, how to stop armoring your heart, you're given this gift of teachings in the form of your life to give you everything you need to open further.*[28] ~ Pema Chödrön

In other words, the world reflects to you the lessons you need to learn. Sometimes, if it feels like the same thing happens over and over, it's because you have something to learn, but you are getting in your own way. You can't see the forest through the trees. You are looking at the flaws in yourself and your life, without pulling back to see the bigger picture and the beauty that's within and all around you. The world is a mirror, trying to show you what you need to learn. In that mirror, our greatest teachers will come to us with lessons. Our greatest teachers aren't necessarily the literal ones from whom we take classes. Rather, they may be the short-tempered store clerk challenging your kindness, the traffic challenging your patience, the weather challenging your expectations, the rude family member challenging your compassion, and your inner critic challenging your ability to love unconditionally. Your guru (teacher) is not in one being. Your guru is everyone and everything you allow.

Jesus acknowledged planting a seed of wisdom in story form to encourage people to learn the often overlooked lessons.

> *That is why I use these parables, For they look, but they don't really see. They hear, but they don't really listen or understand.*
> ~ Matthew 13:13

How can you learn to open your eyes and ears and understand the truth of what's in your world mirror? It starts with the thoughts in your mind that are crowding out your awareness, that constant barrage of rambling that distracts you again and again.

Try this exercise: Each evening, write down what lessons you learned that day or what you could have learned. (Today, traffic taught me to be patient when circumstances are out of my control.)

Alchemy + Trust = Wisdom

Spiritual alchemy is the process by which we take control of our inner landscape and inspire transformation. It's the process of freeing yourself from what holds you back and cultivating what encourages renewal and exponential inner growth. When I practice and teach spiritual alchemy, I always return to the inner mantra of "I am a powerful creator of my reality." Ultimately, *The Space to Choose* is about realizing that you have the reins to your life and learning how to take control through perspective, patience, and various actions, little by little, one step at a time.

You are not at the mercy of your stress or circumstances, but rather, you can challenge yourself to take the right action, which requires wisdom. You cannot be lured into the ramblings of an egocentric mind and think it has the solution. You cannot listen to a melodramatic heart or knee-jerk reaction from a place of emotion. Your deep instincts and intuitive wisdom will always guide you in the right direction. And so, your work is to discern the difference between the head, the heart, and intuitive wisdom. That takes mindfulness and practice in multiple situations over time.

Cultivating wisdom is also learning to trust. I've found that learning to trust is a challenging practice for many. It's difficult because it involves sitting with what is. It may involve accepting a decision you've made or action you've taken or sitting with a situation that is less than ideal. Trust goes hand in hand with surrender, another word that's profoundly challenging for those who like to be in control.

But isn't being a powerful creator of your own reality the opposite of trust and surrender? Actually, it's not. Being a powerful creator of your reality does not mean that you will get everything you want. It means you will receive exactly what you need to learn, grow, and become the best version of yourself so you can be present and celebrate all your life offers you. To do that, you need to take control over what you can — your attitude and your actions — and learn to soften and let go of the rest. It means to surrender. Sometimes, when you do this, you will get what you want because you'll be getting out of your own way, not forcing, not being complacent, but finding sattva, a path and way of being to return to, again and again.

However, sometimes, you face your ego's worst nightmare. There will be circumstances you don't want, but your response and ability to trust that everything will be as it should be will ultimately determine how you experience your reality. If you get upset and stay upset whenever you don't get what you want, you are essentially a spiritual child throwing a temper tantrum. I don't say this flippantly. How are you to know what is best for you when you are stuck in the past, stuck in your fear, overwhelmed with life, and distracted by ego delights? You can't reasonably expect life to unfold exactly as you wish when so many other lives are intertwined with yours. Other's paths matter, as well as your own, and it's important to realize that sometimes you are just a player in someone else's story.

This is why you must cultivate trust. You must trust in yourself, in others, in the world, in God, and/or the universe because you don't have the whole picture. In Theodore Dreiser's *An American Tragedy*, a young man goes to a Native American chief for advice about his missing father. The chief tries to explain the world's ways to the boy and points to the rug they're sitting on. He asks the boy to turn a corner of the rug over and notice the jumbled, seemingly disorganized threads. The chief says that this is what we see of the world. It appears chaotic. He then asks the boy to notice that when the rug is turned right side up, there's a beautiful pattern. The chief suggests that this is how the world looks to God.[29]

The point is that there's an interrelationship between what you might perceive as chaos and what might really be an ordered, purposeful pattern. Taking a higher perspective and utilizing wisdom is the only way to see this in your life. The act of trusting means that sometimes, you can't see the pattern and interconnectedness, but you know it must be there.

Remind yourself, "I am a powerful creator of my reality." Do what you skillfully can. And then let go. Living this balance between action and inaction will help you find a path of wisdom to which you can return and feel confident.

Wisdom is a complex topic, and we've discussed many ways to cultivate it, from understanding to intention setting, spiritual alchemy, and more. Take a moment to absorb all you've learned and consider what practices you will incorporate into your new self-care habits.

Nurturing Your Bliss

Finally, after considering many esoteric topics, we can now talk about how to fall fully into bliss! No, this isn't about eating chocolate, having sex, or watching comedies, though doing those things in moderation might help contribute to pleasurable moments. In the tradition of the koshas, bliss, the fifth innermost layer of your being, is the innate capability to feel ecstatic joy. This bliss isn't conditional but simply present within each of us.

Have you ever felt a sense of deep joy or contentment for no apparent reason? Maybe you attributed it to the weather, noting a bright blue, cloudless sky, a perfect 72 degrees, and the remnants of a faint rainbow. Suddenly, you feel a smile inside that fills you up to the point of feeling whole despite your challenges. Perhaps you associate an experience like this directly with your circumstances. It may be like the heartfelt sensation that arises deep in your chest when you're surrounded by people you not only love but really like. The kind of bliss I'm referring to is not superficial or a fleeting sense of excitement you get when you buy something new or see the latest rom-com. It's much deeper than that. It can arise when your values or sense of purpose are involved or when you are in connection with others. It can arise in nature or because of nature. And it might sneak in during meditation as a warm feeling of contentment. Believe it or not, we can connect to our bliss anywhere at any time. Here are some suggestions to help you cultivate that ability.

Playfulness

I've heard from countless spiritual teachers that we should "never lose our childlike wonder." In all honesty, why would we want to? Being playful opens you up to joy in even the most mundane moments. And yet, for so many, as they pass into adulthood, a serious kind of reservation accompanies the journey into age. These people wear armor that holds them at arm's distance from playfulness. Maybe they've been told seriousness is part of being responsible. Or perhaps they've just become self-conscious and are worried about being judged by others. In any case, it's a good idea to challenge your ego and practice dropping your seriousness, at least some of the time. Playfulness is something we can all do more of. It doesn't mean you will be careless, flippant, or irresponsible. It means you can practice cultivating more moments of intentional bliss. Remember that life is short, so take time to play. Here are some ideas on practicing playfulness:

Play in the Rain

Leave your umbrella behind and step out into a gentle rain. What's the worst that could happen? You'll get wet. Who cares? And to all you moms out there, being in the rain doesn't make you catch a cold; viruses do that. So splash in puddles, walk, run, dance. Put your bare feet in cool, wet grass and take some deep breaths; it's nature therapy, grounding, and play therapy all at once! Bring a friend and tell yourselves you're going to play and be silly, just as an experiment. If you can bring yourself to do this once, I guarantee it won't be the last time.

Get Down on the Floor

Whether you have a dog or a toddler or can babysit someone else's, get down on the floor and play with them. In fact, mimic them. Animals and young children have no inhibition. They live in the present moment and love to play. It doesn't matter what you do here; what's important is that you don't worry about getting wrinkled or dirty. Don't worry about how silly you look. Open yourself up to play, and simply enjoy yourself and your interaction with another being.

Create Something

I love the paint-n-sip studios that have popped up in the last few years. When you attend an event at one, you can not only paint playfully, but you can also enjoy an adult beverage, if you choose, while you create. This is a fun, playful, and creative activity to do alone or with friends. It's not about producing something art-worthy; it's about sharing the experience with others. Many of these studios double the fun by playing music and offering games during the painting process. Find one near you and give it a try.

If the paint-n-sip studios aren't your cup of tea, you can also try arts and crafts on your own. Thousands of YouTube videos instruct how to create everything from holiday ornaments to centerpieces, doodle drawings, and more. Remember to hold a lighthearted spirit if you choose this as your playful activity, and don't let a perfectionist ego creep in to criticize your creation. The intention is just to have fun.

Writing, for me, has always been a creative outlet. Writing poetry often inspires a playful, present-moment experience that offers me a deep feeling of bliss. I discussed haiku in the chapter on caring for your mental and emotional self. You could try that or attempt another type of poetry writing. Here are suggestions to get started:

- Gather some random objects, like a candle, a pinecone, a pillow, a flower, and a glass of water. Items from nature are great, but anything will do.

- Look at these items and brainstorm or mind-dump words that describe how the objects look and/or make you feel. Some possible words might be: relaxed, cozy, flame, dripping wax, brown, earthy, seeds, trees, bright, cheery, love, compassion, soft, inviting, warm, sleepy, quenched, full, refreshed, wet

- Close your eyes and breathe, then compose phrases with these words or items. You don't have to use all the items or words. And it doesn't have to be perfect. (Cozy candlelight cast warmth in the room, as the flowers he left offered a soft glow of his love. My heart was finally quenched.)

- Keep playing and working with the words until they feel right. Your creation can just be for you. You don't have to share it with anyone else.

If you are a serious artist, writer, craftsperson, poet, or painter, you might try bringing a lightness to your next creation. Ease up on the rules of your craft.

What happens if you freehand something or listen to music as you create? Embody a playful spirit as you step outside your regular methods and try something different. Notice how it feels.

Games

When I was growing up, we played board games for fun, and I still do. Hosting a game night is a fantastic way to cultivate an attitude of playfulness. Just keep it light and not too competitive. Whether you play charades, board games, cards, sing karaoke, or make up a game, this is an opportunity to enjoy face-to-face time engaging with friends. Some might say that online gaming can offer a similar benefit, and maybe it does. But in our increasingly technology-driven world, I advocate for as much present engagement with humans as possible. So, whether you engage in online gaming or not, also include face-to-face gaming for good, old-fashioned fun with friends.

Dance

I've been a ballroom and rhythm dancer for almost 20 years because I feel extreme joy when dancing. But you don't have to dance in a structured way to feel joy. Moving rhythmically to music is something human beings have done for thousands of years. Think of ancient and tribal cultures and their raw, rhythmic dancing around a fire. Imagine Renaissance dancing, couples in formal wear circling around a ballroom. All cultures have styles and practices of dance for various purposes. People dance when they are happy. They dance in ritual and prayer. They dance to express sorrow and grief. Some people might encounter a little inhibiting whisper saying they can't dance or fear that they'll be judged if they do. Just remember that if you listen to that voice again and again, you are robbing yourself of the potential for bliss. It may be challenging to let down your guard and just dance, but it will be worth it. Start by practicing alone. Put in earbuds and listen to your favorite tunes. If necessary, lock yourself alone in a room, then close your eyes and move your body to the music. No one's around, and you aren't even looking at yourself. Just feel and move. If you're so inclined, sing out loud while you move. With a little bit of practice, you might really be able to cut loose, alone and with others. And, by all means, if it feels better to learn structured dancing, then do it. There are so many options: country two-step, rumba, cha-cha, hustle, waltz, foxtrot, salsa, bachata, line dancing, ballet, hip-hop, and more! Take a few classes and open yourself up to a great practice for stress relief and bliss.

Drop your Guard

Being playful is about lowering your defenses. If you want to open yourself to deep bliss, you've got to lighten up. Don't take everything so seriously. Remember the Five Remembrances: I am of the nature to grow old, the nature to have ill health, the nature to die, and the nature to lose people I love. My actions are my only true belongings. Unpleasant things that are outside of our control will happen in life. There's no way to hide from this fact. Being serious won't prevent disaster, but cultivating a spirit of playfulness can help you enjoy your life, even when you're struggling. It's okay to laugh too. So, lighten up! Life contains both pleasant and unpleasant happenings. Creating something a little more pleasant, moment to moment, can enable you to touch a place deep inside that will increase your overall happiness.

Laughter as Medicine

Recent research demonstrates that laughter has both psychological and physiological benefits. We all know how good it feels after having a big belly laugh. Apparently, the more we laugh, the less stressed, depressed, or anxious we feel. Cortisol levels and blood pressure can drop, especially for those who laugh regularly.[30] And in a section dedicated to deep bliss, we must talk about laughter.

Laughter is the mind-body reaction we have when we find something silly or amusing. During and after laughter, we can feel a deep inner joy that can be lasting, depending on the source. While watching funny videos or comedies alone may induce laughter, I want to encourage you to embody laughter organically and set yourself up for laughter in interactions with others.

Laughter Yoga

There is a style of yoga that revolves around laughter, and there are even laughter yoga classes. An instructor guides the class in forced laughter, and thanks to the mirror neurons in our brains, we begin laughing authentically after a short period. After sustaining the laughter for a while, you'll feel as if you've had a workout, and the inner smile remains, even if it's just a chuckle at how silly the practice seems. If laughter yoga is available in your area, I highly recommend trying a class. If you're going through a rough time, attend class at least once a week. The forced laughter might just keep you out of a more serious depressive state.

Humor

Everyone's sense of humor is a little different. What's yours like? Do you enjoy sharing your favorite jokes? Do you have a gentle teasing/self-deprecating type of humor? Do you like to find silliness in everyday mundane happenings? Knowing your humor and how those around you accept it is important. I would recommend treading cautiously if you use sarcasm or profanities. There can be a fine line between being funny and being offensive. How can you utilize your sense of humor every day? When by yourself, laugh about whatever you find amusing. When sharing with others, the key is to know your audience. You might be able to tell an off-color joke to your best friend but not your grandmother. If you're reading this and you are the grandmother or don't find much humor in life, I challenge you to ask yourself why. I also invite you to practice dropping your guard and opening yourself to see the silliness around you. Or at least laugh with the people who are laughing.

Playful Interaction

When I counsel couples, I ask each of them to playfully own their shortcomings. In other words, it's important to have a sense of humor about yourself. While this might be more complicated for people with low confidence or perfectionistic tendencies, it is worth working on for many reasons.

First, if we can laugh at ourselves (while still loving ourselves), we embody gentleness and humility, which, in my opinion, are great ingredients for growth. Second, we invite a lightheartedness that enables us to not take things so seriously, which is a real need in our current culture. Life is short, and most of the time, people have positive intentions, so let's not take everything so personally. Allow for humor and playfulness. Finally, in a relationship, being playful with each other's shortcomings can create a deeper bond and feelings of acceptance. If both partners can have enough of a sense of security to say to themselves, *I am loved just as I am, even though I'm not perfect or have this silly tendency*, love grows, and conflict wanes. Let me give you an example.

I'm generally a very ambitious, disciplined person, sometimes to my own detriment. My husband has lovingly devised a term for when I bite off more than I can chew. He calls it "crack mode." He uses this term instead of getting irritated with me. For example, on a weekend day we had free, I said, "Okay, let's go for a walk, then I want to go to Home Depot and buy lumber to build shelves, then when we come back, I'll write in my book a while and build the shelves, then we can go for a bike ride, watch that movie we wanted to see and maybe go salsa dancing after I make dinner from scratch."

Instead of telling me we can't do it all or that I'm ridiculous and there's no way we can do all that, he simply smiles and says, "Uh-oh. We are in crack mode, aren't we?" Instead of being defensive, I can have a moment of self-awareness, see the silliness of my overly energetic tendency, and respond, "Yes! We can do it all!" Generally, we laugh and then pare down the activities to a reasonable number.

I playfully tease my husband because he gets so focused on one thing at a time that I can't engage him in a side conversation or mention something off-topic until that task is completed. Instead of getting mad at him, I understand that this is how his brain works, and I say, "Are you stuck in a waffle square?" He looks up with self-awareness and smiles, saying, "Yes, I am. I need to soak up all the syrup in this one before moving to another one. Leave me in my square!"

We have other playful interactions where we tease ourselves and each other about our natural tendencies and growth edges. The key to this kind of playful interaction is that you must know what buttons are not okay to push, or this practice could go downhill really fast. In other words, we know each other's sensitives, and we would never playfully poke in these areas.

The point is that if you can playfully interact around some personality quirks, it will ward off arguments and irritations. Rather than quarrel, you can laugh together, feel greater love and acceptance, and increase your feelings of deep bliss.

Power of the Pause

Bliss is more than just pleasure and humor. It can be a simple yet profound feeling of contentment. When we practice mindfulness, even for a moment, we can enter a state of bliss with appreciation for that little nugget of time. Try this exercise: Bring your awareness to your feet without moving them. Feel the soles of your feet. Think of how your feet support you, ground you, move you from place to place. Imagine the curves of your feet, all your toes, your heels, and the tops of your feet. Allow your feet to relax deeply. Now, take a deep breath. Relax your whole body. Soften everything. Feel the softening.

What did that very brief exercise feel like? Taking just a mindful moment can reduce feelings of stress and anxiety and increase feelings of contentment. A pause can break a pattern of negative thinking and allow for a hard reset. So, remember the pause and use it to feel a moment of bliss.

Gratitude

The importance of gratitude bears repeating as we consider nurturing our bliss. While gratitude can help shift our attitude, improve mental and emotional health, uplift our energy, and make us more mindful, it can also encourage feelings of contentment that lead us to embody our most blissful state of being. You can practice the 30-day gratitude journal and also make gratitude a spur-of-the-moment practice. I've started to include space for gratitude at the end of every meditation, reminding myself of what I'm most grateful for. This starts my day in a joyful place where I feel unflappable.

On your worst days, practicing gratitude can help balance the emotional heaviness you might otherwise be feeling. Say something to yourself like, *I am sad that these things happened, but I'm grateful for my home and the love I have in my life.*

It's not either or. We can learn to hold space for both the sorrow and the joy at the same time. In doing so, we are remembering and fueling this deep inner bliss that's present within all of us. And that makes the challenging times seem like passing storms.

Fruits of the Holy Spirit

Several years ago, I conducted a yoga teacher training program at The Brain Health Center, founded by Dr. Paul Nussbaum. It was an integrative facility that offered neuro-psych testing, nutrition, massage, acupuncture, counseling, yoga, ballet, and more. They had a beautiful studio in the back, with windows all around, and these words painted on the walls: love, joy, peace, patience, kindness, goodness, faithfulness, gentleness, self-control. Seeing the words surrounding us while I taught warmed my heart. We were trying to embody and live all of those words.

One day, I asked Paul's wife, Kim, who was the studio manager, how she chose those particular words for the studio walls. She smiled and told me, "They're the fruits of the Holy Spirit." She had to explain further, as I was not as familiar with the Bible, that it was from Galatians 5:22. "As we get closer to God," she said, "these qualities are enhanced."

I imagine that embodying love, joy, peace, patience, kindness, goodness, faithfulness, gentleness, and self-control would indeed help one get closer to the divine and bring deep feelings of spiritual bliss and contentment. I keep a little card with these inspirational words printed on it to help me remember the fruits of the Holy Spirit and remember what I'm working toward.

Visualization of Light

When I experience pain, either physical or emotional, I work with a visualization of light during meditation. I imagine it filling me from top to bottom, or sometimes, the light emanates from my center and radiates outward. If I have physical pain, I focus on the light swirling around in this area, smoothing it out and healing it from the inside. Some might say what I'm doing is energy work like Reiki. Others might say it's silly. But it gives me a sense of control and lifts my spirits. Does this practice help my injuries, or does my heart heal faster? Maybe, maybe not. But it does, I believe, open up a channel to my inner bliss, so it's worth my time. Consider doing a light visualization during meditation or find a guided practice that uses light (I have one on Insight Timer).[31]

Most of all, keep cultivating and nurturing your bliss in all the ways I've mentioned and find new practices that bring you joy and contentment. Bliss is a wonderful human experience; we all could experience more of it.

Forming Good Habits

What practice serves you best? That is the essential question, not: What are you doing now that's habitual, and you like it, but it serves no purpose in terms of self-care, self-love, or self-growth. We all form autopilot habits, and it's not until we seriously investigate what we are doing and why that we will figure out what works for us. You might already go to the gym three to five times a week, and maybe you meditate just as often. But when life gets really stressful or an unforeseen event occurs, you may feel a wreck inside. Your current practices aren't enough. Or maybe they aren't the "right" practices for you in stressful times. So you need to shift. How can you use your time differently and more effectively? Maybe you need to socialize, journal, go into the woods, call on your strengths, or try to tap into your inner wisdom.

Many people get frustrated with the idea of self-care because they say they have no time. However, we all get the same 24 hours. Consider being honest with yourself regarding what you are doing with yours.

Prioritize

What is most important to you when it comes to all the topics we've discussed in Part Three? What are your baseline practices to keep yourself going? This will be different for all of us, even though I think everyone should be eating healthy, exercising, and meditating. Maybe being in nature is number one for you, or maybe you need to have daily social engagement. The key to forming good habits is first figuring out what your priorities are and then creating boundaries around them. Setting boundaries means that those priorities are non-negotiable parts of your self-care, and you won't sabotage yourself by choosing other tasks, distractions, or even people instead of completing your essential practices. If you don't set priorities for yourself, you are draining rather than filling your cup.

Discipline

Being disciplined requires a strong resolve driven by motivation. It means that you do your best, and you know that your best might look different from day to day, but you keep going. Some people might be born with discipline or learn it from their parents and environment at a young age. Some might have to teach themselves discipline later in life as they work toward an important goal. If you struggle with discipline, here are some tips to get you started.

Schedule

Being disciplined involves creating a schedule for yourself and adhering to it. You already have a schedule of some sort, a series of habits you practice every day, whether you realize it or not. You wake up. Perhaps you shower first. Then you make yourself some coffee. Then, you read your email. The question to ask yourself is, does this serve me and my goals, or could I shift my morning routine to match what's important to me? Change is not easy, especially when your routine is deeply ingrained in habit. But the first step is making one little shift, maybe just a few days a week. Then, you can compare your new routine to your old one and see which serves you best. A wellness coach can help you with this if it's hard to do it alone.

Community

Practicing good habits in a community can offer you great support for getting started or keeping you on track. Yoga and meditation retreats have always served to refresh my home practices. On retreat, you usually follow a schedule: 6:30 am yoga class, 8:15 am breakfast, post-breakfast hike, free time until lunch, etc. When you can step away from life's responsibilities and just consider your own well-being, you learn what brings you mental/emotional steadiness and physical wellness. Then, you can take this information home with you to fit it into your everyday schedule.

Attending exercise classes, meditation groups, spiritual groups, book clubs, and other intentional gatherings can help keep you on track because you can share your experiences, your triumphs and struggles, and know you're not alone. This sense of community can help you find greater resolve to continue with the practices that support you.

Reflection

Whether you're shifting your habits on your own or have a coach or community to assist you, taking time periodically to reflect and assess is essential. Try not to use reflection time to beat yourself up or tell yourself you're not good enough. Be as objective as possible. Recognize what you have accomplished and pause to be grateful for that. Then, reassess if something doesn't seem to be working. Ask yourself if it's the activity, the time of day, being legitimately busy, unexpected circumstances, or your mindset that's holding you back. Make any necessary adjustments to your schedule and try again.

Sample Self-Care Schedule

Many years ago, a teacher of mine recommended we write out the self-care practices we plan to do daily, weekly, bi-monthly, monthly, bi-annually, and annually. This model has served me well in helping me see that I don't have to do everything all at once; rather, care is woven throughout my life. Punah punah. This kind of schedule also affords many opportunities to shift anytime it's necessary.

Daily Practice

Give yourself at least one hour per day as a reasonable starting place; it could be in two 30-minute chunks or three 20-minute chunks. These times are merely a starting place. Your daily practice may look very different from what I am suggesting. In any case, challenge yourself to incorporate different categories of self-care into your schedule.

- MINDFULNESS: Sit and practice mindfulness or breathing techniques of your choice for 10-15 minutes a day. This is the minimum amount of practice time required to have a positive effect on the brain and nervous system, and it is also a doable amount of time. If you're able to sit for longer, go ahead; you'll benefit from longer sessions. And if you need to split those 10 minutes into two five-minute sessions, that's okay, too. Just make sure you're taking time every day for your own mental, emotional, physical, and spiritual well-being. (10-15 minutes)

- MOVEMENT: Perhaps this is different every day; choices might be walking, hiking, running, yoga, weights, Pilates, HITT, dance, or whatever you enjoy. (30 minutes)

- READING & REFLECTION: Maybe this is time to read a wisdom text, journal, practice gratitude, or cultivate positivity by engaging in a little laughter (15-20 minutes)

- MOMENTS: Try to have moments of awareness where you can breathe deep, look at the sky, be grateful, laugh, find wisdom, or stretch. These kinds of actions can be woven into your day. They don't have to be something on your to-do list.

Weekly (Or Bi-Weekly) Practice

Try incorporating something extra into your wellness routine each week or two.

- MINDFULNESS: Consider a special weekly practice that involves mindfulness. Perhaps you could take a yoga or qigong class or take a solo walk in the woods to find a seat in nature for some shinrin-yoku (forest bathing). Maybe your weekly practice involves taking more time to read inspirational or spiritual books or articles that resonate with you. You could journal what you've learned in the past week or what you're grateful for. Taking a little extra time once a week to deepen your mindfulness mindset will help reinforce your daily practice and help you control your stress levels with greater ease.

- MOVEMENT: Consider taking a different physical activity class or joining a friend in an activity to make it fun and switch up your routine. Try dance, Pilates, hiking, pickleball or whatever you're curious about. You might try something different, like horseback riding or salsa dancing on the weekend, as those activities might fit your schedule better at that time.

- WELLNESS PREP: Take some time to prepare healthy meals and plan your week's tasks. Readjust your schedule as necessary and try to eliminate at least one non-essential thing from your schedule. Don't fill that space with anything but your own self-care.

Monthly (Or Bi-Monthly) Practice

Once a month or so, you could try an additional approach to self-care.

- MINDFULNESS: Once a month, commit to a longer formal and informal practice. Maybe on the first Sunday morning of the month, you could sit and meditate for 30 minutes. Alternatively, you could journal or attend a class. Focus on clearing your mind.

- MOVEMENT & WELLNESS: Learn a new skill or revisit a flow activity. Be creative, musical, artistic, or use a skill or ability you don't practice regularly. See your therapist, get a massage, acupuncture, or other holistic service. Take time to do your personal grooming: haircuts, nails, etc. And give your physical space a good deep clean of your home or reorganize. These things are important, too, as they create a sense of order, confidence, and clarity.

- REFLECTION & COMMUNITY: Consider a deeper dive of awareness into yourself. Start a new psychology, self-help, or spiritual book, or read some inspirational articles. Reflect on where you are and whether you are on a path that feels right. Give yourself time monthly to assess all the areas of your life to see if they are aligned with the values you want to live by. And if you haven't done it the rest of the month, connect with your community, whether it's friend groups, spiritual groups, or family. Or perhaps you could host a game night to bring your community together for some laughs.

Annually (Or Bi-Annually)

Once a year, take a step back, evaluate your self-care, and offer yourself the opportunity for something special.

- MINDFULNESS: If your budget and schedule allow, I highly recommend a minimum of two trips per year. Make one of these a retreat. It can be a simple getaway as part of a meditation group, yoga group, church group, writing group, or "whatever you're interested in" group. Make sure your getaway is in a peaceful place where you focus on rest and a healing activity of your choosing; be mindful about being mostly or completely unplugged. Also, plan a trip to a new place that's on your bucket list. Enjoy yourself there, take friends, family, and kids, and again, try to remain mostly unplugged. Be present. Have fun.

- MOVEMENT: Some people like to work toward a goal with exercise, like running a 5k or half marathon, entering a dance competition, getting a black belt, or achieving something else. Having an annual goal can help keep you on track throughout the year, as you're always training both for the present moment and for the future.

- WELLNESS: Schedule and attend all of your regular wellness appointments, doctors, dentists, and any other specialists you see every six months or year. Consider treating yourself with an extra holistic session you don't ordinarily do, such as Reiki, acupuncture, or essential oil therapy. Try something new and pamper yourself.

With these examples in mind, devise written daily, weekly, monthly, and yearly self-care goals according to a schedule that makes sense for you.

Part Four: Connection

(Presence & Communication)

Most living things have systems of connection and ways of supporting and communicating with each other. Trees in the forest, for example, have an underground fungal network called mycelium that allows them to share water, nutrients, and more. German forester and author Peter Wohlleben coined this network the "wood-wide web" because it is through mycelium that trees "communicate" with each other.[32]

Bees have an elaborate communication system to enable them to gather pollen and protect the queen. Flowers encourage connection with pollinators by growing in attractive colors and shapes. Whales, other mammals, birds, plants, and micro-ecosystems connect and communicate. In truth, our entire world is connected and communicating, whether we realize it or not.

Connection and communication between humans are essential for our survival in many ways. Connecting can be so simple, and like many things, we can make it very complicated. Ultimately, we all want to be seen, to be heard and understood, and to be loved unconditionally. We often go to great lengths to attain this kind of connection, sometimes without even knowing we are doing it.

In tribal communities, connection is created through the clothes and colors worn, the dances performed, and the songs sung. We do the same in Western culture. Fashion, for example, is simply a way for us all to connect, as if to say, *you're like me, and I'm like you if we wear the same style.* When we belong to a book club, a yoga class, an athletic team, a sorority, or even a family, it's a way of fitting in, as if we were all doing the same dance or singing the same song. And when circumstances in our lives change, and we can't buy the latest gadget or fashion (to fit in), or the group we belong to breaks up, we sometimes feel lost and alone, though we might not realize why.

Building connections with other people is a part of finding meaning and purpose in life. Who do you feel the most connected to? Is it your best friend, significant other, parent, sibling, or someone else? Your special "person" could even be your dog. If you're lucky, perhaps you have many special connections in your life. Regardless of who your special person is, think about how that connection came to be.

We certainly feel connected to those we spend time with. But how do deeper feelings of connection develop? Perhaps deeper connections arise due to similar interests or humor, stage of life commonality, physical attraction (not necessarily sexual), dependability, feelings of compassion, admiration, or something else. Some say feeling in tune with someone reflects a spiritual connection; they feel like soul friends. And then there's family. Of course, they've seen you through ups and downs and hopefully will support you no matter what.

But what about developing deep connections in other contexts? I've done several silent retreats, in which a group comes together to be quiet in reflection, meditation, or prayer. I often don't know these people, yet I always feel connected to them after the retreat. If I run into them afterward, I give them a warm embrace like they were old friends. Even though our days of sharing space were in silence, I feel like I know them. Is this feeling of connection due to the shared experience? A spiritual link? Non-verbal communication? Simple presence? Perhaps it's a combination of all these elements.

I've been a part of the ballroom and Latin dance community in my local area for many years. Dozens of people gather from all walks of life to learn and practice dance together. For the most part, we don't talk; we dance. As we dance together, we engage in shared present-moment awareness and extensive nonverbal communication. The practice of dance itself brings me so much joy, but so does the spirit and energy of the people. I feel connected to the dance community. Do you have a community you feel connected to?

We know that satisfying social connection is vital to overall well-being. Research shows that it will not only improve long-term mental, emotional, and physical health outcomes, but it can also increase longevity.[33] This means we must be mindful of and cultivate connections for a fulfilling life. Part Four: Connection is the final section of *The Space to Choose* because, ideally, we need to practice awareness and self-control (Mindfulness), get to know ourselves (Discovery), and learn to love ourselves (Care) before we can successfully cultivate connections with others. My goal is to offer you techniques and wisdom to assist and inspire you on your journey toward deeper, more satisfying relationships. As we explore facets of connection, which include nonverbal and verbal communication, I'll guide you, support you, and challenge your habitual ways of being so that you can have more fulfilling experiences in your life.

Technology as a Potential Roadblock

Connection, the present-moment experience of sharing space with another being, can result in a profound sense of meaning. Unfortunately, technological distractions often prevent meaningful connections from occurring. As technology grows with great fervor, we are experiencing a slow loss of our direct human connection. Although social media and messaging apps might make people feel somewhat connected, we can still feel isolated, even in the same room. How frequently do you see a couple out at dinner, and both of them are on their phones? Are you one of those couples? Many say technology makes work easier, which it might, but what are you doing with your newfound free time? Working more? There are greater demands on us professionally than ever before because of those little glowing rectangles in our hands. We are at everyone's disposal 24 hours a day, seven days a week. This means we might not always be paying attention to the people and places right in front of us. People watch concerts through the lens of their phones, post on social media while on a hike or vacationing in beautiful locations, and bring their laptops to family picnics to catch up on their email. During the COVID-19 pandemic, we found that social isolation accompanied solely by virtual interaction exacerbated the already growing mental health crisis. Clearly, we can't let technology replace genuine human connection.

I'm not anti-technology. Responsible use of technology tools can be incredibly beneficial, but we must be cautious. We don't want to diminish our ability to create meaning, art, purpose, and connection. We don't want to distance ourselves from each other, nature, or our sense of spirituality and purpose. These abilities and bonds don't come from the artificial world, and the connection you think you feel on social media isn't as fulfilling as a real-life relationship. Of course, a connection can exist from a distance. Great love stories tell us about couples who were separated due to circumstances and keep their love alive through letters, emails, phone calls, and Zoom. I'm certainly not discounting that. However, it is also important to have people who are physically present in your life with whom you can connect and on whom you can depend.

Can you imagine anyone whose dying wish was to spend more time at the office or on social media? What would you regret not doing if your time to die were near? Let's be skillful with our time and energy so we can offer ourselves the most beautiful and fulfilling life. To do this, start by considering the following questions. Take time to either ponder them or write in a journal.

- What does connection mean to you?

- When did you last feel connected to another human being, a group, or yourself?

- How lasting is that connection? Was it momentary, or has it been sustained?

- With whom or what do you want to build a greater connection?

Make a list of connections that are most important to you. Maybe it's your family, friends, community, pets, nature, or place of worship. Maybe it's just one person. Knowing is the first step in skillful connection building.

Nonverbal Communication

Much of connection is nonverbal. While the words we use to express ourselves are quite significant, and we will be discussing how to be better verbal communicators, this is not the only way we communicate. Most experts agree that around 80-90% of all communication is non-verbal.

Let's go back to our dog being our best friend. The dog never speaks to you. Or does she? I know my dog is an amazing communicator. She's my therapy companion, and without a word, she knows when to put her head in the lap of someone in distress, "Pet me, and you'll feel better," she says. I never taught her to do that. She also knows when it's time for dinner, when we will take a walk (before I say anything), and when I'm about to leave (she requests extra attention and a goodbye kiss). She even communicates confusion, for instance, when I host a Halloween party and people come dressed in costumes. Her eyes tell me she loves me when we are relaxed and sitting together. And she lets the dog sitter know exactly what cabinet the treats are in so I don't have to tell her. When I am sad, especially if I shed tears, she throws her whole body onto me for a hug and some snuggles; she knows her fur is comforting to pet and will make me feel better.

Communication is more than words. When I sit in nature, practicing shinrin-yoku, I often ask the trees what they can teach me. I look up at them, and I know the answer, "Weather the storm," "Be patient," "Learn to let go." Are the trees speaking these phrases to me? Certainly not. But I feel they live as an example of these concepts, and if I slow down enough and am observant, I receive this wisdom simply by being in the presence of these living giants. This is an example of connection in nature.

When my husband and I are at a gathering, we can communicate with a glance from across the room, letting each other know that either we are relaxed and having fun, one of us needs saving from the conversation we are in, or it's time to go. How do we do that without planning signals beforehand? Because we are connected, and we know each other's nonverbal body language.

Strengthening your nonverbal skills involves understanding both the messages you're sending and learning how to read others' body language. It doesn't have to involve memorizing and practicing specific movements or gestures. There are many books available on body language and nonverbal communication if you're interested in delving into interpretations on the subject. In my opinion, however, you can begin to learn more about body language with simple mindfulness practice.

Mindful Observation

In Part One: Mindfulness, we discussed the importance of self-awareness and self-control. Mindful observation is essential when considering connection and communication. We have to be able to see clearly. If you pause just for a breath or two to clear your mind and center yourself, you will be more prepared to see clearly and connect with someone in the present moment.

Notice Your Inner State

First, you must observe and center yourself before talking with someone. Ask yourself if you have time or can be present with this person or in this setting. You can't see clearly and observe nonverbal behavior if you are only half paying attention. Ask yourself if you can put aside distractions like your phone or thoughts about your to-do list and give this person your full attention. Do an internal check-in by noticing your body and how it feels, your energy level, your mood, and what's on your mind. If you cannot get something off your mind, you might ask the person in front of you to give you a few minutes to send a message or write something down so you can address it later. (If it's not a good time to chat, you might reschedule a big conversation, but try not to postpone it for more than 24 hours, or the person you are talking with might feel unimportant.) Ground yourself in the moment by taking a deep breath, feeling your feet on the floor, and telling yourself that you are here in the present moment and nothing else matters. Then, sit or stand with an open posture that communicates you are ready to receive what the other person has to offer.

Observe Their State

Next, explore the person in front of you (or the setting you're in) with your eyes. Slow down to access wisdom and notice any natural perceptions that come to you when observing this person. Notice their posture, their energy, their emotional state, and their level of attention. In general, how will this person be able to sit with you in the present moment? Allow your observations to be as clear and unbiased as possible before you engage with the person in front of you. What we perceive might not always be accurate, but the more we practice mindful seeing when we ourselves are grounded, the better our observations will become.

Often, we are solely focused on ourselves, and we don't notice someone else's state of being. Arguments and misunderstandings can occur when we choose the wrong time to discuss something because we miss the cues that tell us someone is already distressed. It's important to slow down and be observant each time you engage with someone.

Notice these four things about them: their posture, energy, emotion, and attention. These are the same internal awareness elements you use on yourself; you're simply attempting to observe them in another. Try to notice the facts without adding judgment, assumption, or a story to what you observe. This takes practice and the ability to discern fact from story. The more you practice mindfulness, the easier it will be to cultivate the ability to observe.

Body Language

As you learn to stay grounded, you'll naturally be able to read someone's body language. As you increase your awareness of body language, you may find opportunities to make positive changes in your own nonverbal communication. Here are some tips to look for and use when connecting nonverbally:

Facial Expression

We have over 40 muscles in our faces alone. This is how facial expressions convey so many emotions. Without a word, you can see if someone is curious, stressed, happy, relaxed, frustrated, angry, tense, or playful.

A genuine smile, probably the loveliest thing to see on another person, is often contagious. You know if a smile is genuine because little crinkles appear around the eyes. Someone can fake a smile, but their eyes usually won't be involved. Notice this in others and yourself when you are joyful rather than trying to offer a polite smile without a real feeling behind it.

You can observe someone's jaw and mouth to determine if they are stressed because muscles around the sides of the cheeks often tense up or the lips appear tightly pursed together. This could also indicate that someone is frustrated, disappointed, or angry.

All the little muscles around the eyes enable the eyes to be very expressive. Solid eye contact can indicate interest and curiosity, but intense staring can mean someone intends to dominate or intimidate. A slightly furrowed forehead, with a little line between the eyebrows, can indicate concern or worry. Lifted eyebrows usually show surprise or disbelief. And feelings of love or kindness create a softening around the eyes.

The more you start to watch people's facial expressions, the more you'll be able to intuit the emotions behind them.

Posture

Many of us don't have the best posture due to lifestyles that involve sitting in front of a computer for hours and being on our phones for the rest of the time. However, a person's particular posture provides significant nonverbal signals to what they may be feeling and how best to connect with them.

In general, an open posture indicates being comfortable and confident. Closed posture indicates disinterest or defensiveness. So, when people cross their arms, they may feel defensive or angry. Conversely, think about people who seem to be trying to take up a lot of physical space by standing tall with arms open wide (or in a Superman/woman position with hands on hips). In this case, they may just be confident, or they could be trying to dominate the conversation or situation. A slumped posture can indicate timidity, uncertainty, or even fear. If you observe these postures, it's important to keep your own posture relaxed and open. This is certainly true if someone takes an aggressive stance. Think of two bucks in the wild, standing off right before a fight. If you encourage the fight or flight trigger in the other person, the communication will deteriorate quickly, no matter what words are said. It's usually best to have your arms at your sides or loosely in your lap and sit tall with your legs uncrossed, softening through your neck, shoulders, and face.

Physically mirroring those you speak with can also help you connect. Cross your legs the way they cross theirs and lean to the side with your elbow on the chair arm if that's what they're doing. They'll feel more understood by you before you say a word. Of course, if the other person exhibits extreme emotional nonverbal posture, as in a fight or flight reaction, you do not want to mirror that.

Gestures

Most of us speak with our hands in some way, whether just waving them in the air as we tell a story or more subtly clenching our fists when stressed. These are also good cues to notice when considering your body language or someone else's. Some people pick at their fingernails or cuticles if they feel anxious. Others squeeze something or fidget when nervous or overwhelmed. Pay attention to what you do with your hands when talking to someone, then notice others.

I've given you a very general overview of basic body language. Many books explore this topic more deeply if you're interested. The key is to use this information not only to observe other people's nonverbal cues but, first and foremost, to consider your own. What unintended messages are you sending? It's worth reprogramming your autopilot if it's not serving you to be an effective communicator or helping you to make deeper connections.

Touch

Touch, something we require as human beings, is part of nonverbal communication. My husband has learned that when I'm distressed, usually the less he says, the better. But if he holds my hand or hugs me, I feel supported and often much lighter. Touch, both comforting touch and touch that leads to sexual intimacy, is essential for couples. Most experts agree that couples who are physically distant from each other don't usually stay together long-term.

We all need touch. It starts as babies as we seek the comforting feeling of being close. The fussiest little ones will often be soothed when they're held to mom's or dad's chest. As our children grow, they need to be hugged and their boo-boos kissed. Affection can be very healing. Even our pets crave a good belly rub or scratch behind the ears as a way of connecting with us. Most mammals live in packs and sleep closely huddled together; it's in our nature. Animals enjoying affection from each other is the stuff of social media reels, with dogs and cats seeking each other for snuggles.

It's an unfortunate time we are in, post-COVID-19, where everyone got somewhat used to physical distance, and now we sometimes hesitate to shake hands, let alone hug. We also sometimes hesitate with touch because we are more aware than ever of the widespread incidences of trauma, much of which can create a sense of potential violation or fear around being touched.

Scientifically speaking, touch, especially hugging, is important. Hugs release oxytocin (a feel-good hormone) and can dramatically reduce feelings of tension and anxiety. Hugging can create feelings of trust and safety and can even boost your immune system.[34] They cultivate connection when welcomed.

But not every situation is appropriate for a hug. A simple touch of the hand or hand on the shoulder can offer a reassuring connection to help someone in distress. While I want to encourage you to touch those close to you as a means of connection, if you ever doubt what is appropriate, simply ask permission, "Is it okay if I put my hand on your shoulder?" "Would you like a hug?" Before carrying out the touch, mindfully observe the person's physical reaction to your ask. If they look closed off, not opening their arms to receive a hug, it might be best to hold back, even if they said "sure" to your request.

Sometimes, people say "yes" out of obligation, and it's not what they need or want. If you're ever on the receiving end of such a request, know that it is always okay to politely decline. "No thank you" is a complete statement. You don't have to explain further. Again, while I primarily want to discuss how important touch can be in creating connection, I also want you to remember that everyone should have a choice in giving and receiving affection, and that includes children. In my childhood, it wasn't uncommon for parents to "force" their kids to hug everyone, even when they very clearly felt uncomfortable hugging. Everyone (as young as possible) needs to develop physical autonomy over what they do and don't do with their bodies.

If you find that you are closed off to affection from everyone in your life, it might be worth exploring why. While it might not be a high priority for everyone, affection is a natural part of life and relationships. However, if you have experienced trauma, especially as a child, your brain might be subconsciously wired to view affection as something threatening. A good therapist can help you work through such feelings so you can work toward enjoying connecting touch. Then, with friends and family, when you feel comfortable, ask for a hug or to sit close when you need to. And snuggle up with your pets if you have them.

Intention

There's a saying about the road to hell being paved with good intentions. This is why following through with the actions that support those intentions is so important. I previously quoted Mahatma Gandhi saying, "happiness is when what we think, what we say, and what we do are all in harmony." I'm repeating it now because it is a key concept in mindfulness, self-discovery, self-care, and in building connections with others.

Consider the nonverbal signals you send if you have negative thoughts about someone but then offer them a "fake" interaction, pretending to be interested in or to like them. You might think you're good at pretending, but people can usually feel your inner attitude, even if subconsciously. Have you interacted with someone and felt that something was "off"? Perhaps it was because their outer presentation was dissonant with their inner thoughts and intentions. This doesn't mean you should treat someone poorly because you are cranky and want to say you are authentic. The point is to work on your attitude before engaging with others so you can connect with them authentically.

Try sending a negative person you know a positive thought or saying a prayer for them before you have an interaction. Notice how you feel doing so and how the person receives your interaction. When our thoughts and intentions align with our actions, not only do we feel better, as we are in harmony, but people perceive us as being more genuine because we *are* more genuine.

Having trouble mustering up a positive thought or intention for someone who irritates you? Try this Loving Kindness Meditation. It's a great way to cultivate gentleness for yourself first, to attempt an attitude shift towards others.

There are four statements. First, you say them for yourself (silently or aloud). Offer these words to yourself with heartfelt intention:
May I be safe.
May I be happy and content.
May I be as healthy as possible in this moment.
May I live with ease.

Next, you repeat the phrases for someone you love as you picture them in your mind's eye:
May you be safe.
May you be happy and content.
May you be as healthy as possible in this moment.
May you live with ease.

Then, you repeat those same four phrases for someone neutral to you (e.g.: the postal carrier, coffee barista, grocery store clerk). Finally, you repeat the phrases for someone who challenges you, annoys you, or with whom you have real struggles. That last one can be difficult, for sure. You might start by saying the phrases through gritted teeth. But think about it this way: if that difficult person in your life felt safe, happy, healthy, and lived with ease, would they be miserable or hurt you as they have? Probably not. So, that's a reason to wish it for them. Many people I know, including myself, have changed the nature of a relationship with a difficult person in their lives by doing this meditation practice. Remember, the only thing we have control over is ourselves. So, if we can shift our attitude, and I mean truly shift how we feel inside, it will also be reflected outside. People will feel it, and they will respond to you differently.

> *When I'm unsure, when I'm confused, I check my motivation. If my motivation is pure, I don't care what anybody thinks about me. If my motivation is afflictive—that's to say, it uses emotional fuels that are not benevolent, such as spite, envy, hate, impatience, intolerance, or superiority—then I know I have to work on myself.* [36]
> ~ *The Dalai Lama*

Intention matters. Our inner story and attitude matter. If you frequently feel irritated or grumpy, consider that the feeling is coming from inside of you. It's not everyone or everything else's fault that you are cranky. Address that feeling inside, and use your mindfulness tools to recognize and heal your internal pain so you can approach the world with greater equanimity. You'll have control over your intention, and you'll be able to nonverbally connect with others more authentically.

In summary, there are many components to nonverbal communication, some of which are body language, which we can learn to pay closer attention to with mindful observation; touch, which we can practice giving and receiving in healthy, supportive ways; and intention, which involves an internal attitude shift that may enhance interpersonal connections.

Emotional Connection

We bond over shared experiences, particularly ones that are emotionally charged. Think of how it feels to be in the home stands of a sports team that is having a winning season. Or to sit in an ancient European chapel during a religious service. How about the feeling in a comedy club when a stellar comedian is cracking jokes? In those moments, you may have felt connected even to the strangers sitting near you.

Human beings can experience big emotions, and we are capable of feeling each other's enthusiasm or heaviness during powerful emotional moments. Think about what a holiday is like around your family's table. There may be lots of laughter and lightness or overwhelming tension and reserve. If there's been a tragedy or loss, you may feel grief. You've probably sensed all these feelings at one time or another.

Empaths

Do you know someone who is frequently chipper or frequently grumpy? Notice if your mood shifts the next time you're around that person. People's emotional energy can rub off on those nearby. You might not even be aware of it until you start to pay attention. People who are particularly sensitive to others' emotions are often referred to as empaths. They don't just notice other people's emotions; they can almost feel them as their own. While this can be great if you're around someone joyful, it's tough if you're around someone who is in pain (most grumpy people are so because they are in either physical or emotional pain). If you are an empath, it's important to learn emotional and energetic boundaries. Here are some tips:

- Check-in with your own emotions frequently throughout the day. Ask yourself, "How do I feel right now?"

- When engaging with another person, try to be mindful if your mood or emotions shift from what they were since your last check-in. If they shift, ask yourself, "Is this my emotion?"

- After engaging with someone and experiencing a mood shift, practice the "brush off." Stand up. Start by bringing your opposite hand to the top of your opposite shoulder, then sweep down your arm all the way to the palm of your hand as if you were trying to brush off a cobweb. Repeat several times on that side before moving to the other side. Continue brushing off down your chest, belly, lower back, and down the legs (all sides) to the feet. Do this as if you had a residue of some sort all over your clothes and you were trying to brush it off. While you brush off, take deep breaths, in through the nose and out through the mouth. When you're finished, come into stillness and notice how you feel.

- It's also important for empaths (and everyone) to practice grounding techniques: come into stillness and feel your feet rooting into the ground. Or stand outside in the grass or dirt with no shoes on. "Plant yourself" in the present moment. Meditate.

Doing these things often will help keep you balanced and aware of yourself and your emotions so that you can still feel connected to other people and enjoy that emotional connection without taking on their feelings as if they were your own.

Non-Empaths

There are many articles written about empaths and HSPs (highly sensitive persons), but not much is written about those who aren't "big feelers." While it is certainly okay to not take on other people's emotions or feel them in a big way, some level of empathy is an important skill for all human beings to cultivate. And, while the opposite of an empath is a narcissist (someone who is too self-centered to care about someone else's feelings), not everyone who is a non-empath is a narcissist. Remember that these concepts and terms always fall on a spectrum; they are not either/or personality descriptors. Some people are more logic-oriented and less emotion-focused. That doesn't mean they don't care about people's feelings, and it doesn't mean they don't have feelings; it means they process the world very differently than people who are more empathic or emotional. If you fall into the more logic-focused and less empathic category, it is essential for you to develop understanding and sensitivity toward your own and other people's feelings. Here are some ways to cultivate emotional connection.

- Practice noticing your own emotions first. Internally, say to yourself, *I feel...* then notice if an emotion word comes to mind. If you're struggling to find an emotion word, try choosing one from this list: frustrated, overwhelmed, irritated, angry, disgusted, scared, confused, uncertain, sad, heavy, depressed, neutral, light, happy, joyful, satisfied, curious, humorous, wonder-filled, excited, elated. It is okay if your word is "neutral" for a while. If you practice asking yourself daily, you might notice other feelings emerge occasionally. You don't have to change them. Your job is to just notice them and label them.

- Practice mindful observation of others. Try to determine someone's current emotion based on body language. Notice the person's posture, facial expression, and hand position. If someone looks distressed and the situation is appropriate, you might ask how they feel. Do not try to guess their feelings (out loud) or say that they look a certain way. With genuine interest, simply say, "How are you?"

- Be curious and compassionate. If someone expresses a distressing emotion, practice validating and empathic responses like, "Oh, I hear you. You feel angry about [that circumstance]. I can understand why you feel that way." You don't have to try to solve a problem or fix anything. A little understanding and empathy go a long way to making an emotional connection. Most of us just want to be seen, heard, and understood.

- Consider that some people process the world through feelings, just as you process it through your own mind and logic. As you get familiar with your own big emotions, remember that you're not alone. We all feel a range of emotions. Feelings aren't good or bad; they are just part of our experience.

Learning to be curious about and understanding feelings is paramount to practical and spiritual development. It is also essential to cultivating connection. The more kindness you can direct towards yourself in challenging emotional situations, the more compassion you will be able to genuinely offer someone else.

Sharing Emotions

Laughter reflects positive emotions like joy or happiness and can be a reaction to funny or mildly embarrassing circumstances. Laughing strengthens social bonds and releases dopamine, serotonin, and endorphins. All these feel-good hormones can enhance motivation, create overall feelings of wellness, and even decrease pain. There are many ways to invite laughter into your life, from good comedy shows to cultivating a playful attitude within close relationships. Sharing laughter with your friends and family will create positive memories and increase feelings of connection, so consider planning fun activities regularly to get giggling together.

On nearly the opposite end of the spectrum, grief is a painful emotional response to loss in life. We must allow ourselves time and space to grieve and feel the losses we experience. Some might do this by crying, journaling, exercising, joining support groups, or seeing a therapist. But sometimes, we repress our grief because it feels simply too much to bear. So we try to bury it inside. Learn to recognize when you are avoiding these kinds of feelings. Signs of avoidance include: constantly busying yourself with work or projects, zoning out on social media or watching videos or movies for far too many hours in the day, or turning to substances like alcohol, drugs, or even junk food to try to soothe the pain you're suppressing. We need to learn to feel and move through our own grief so that we can then see grief in another person and hold space for them or share in the grief together without getting overwhelmed. It's not an easy process. It requires mindful grounding and acceptance of the cycles of life. Everything we've discussed so far can prepare you to experience big emotions, like grief, with less fear and a little more understanding.

You can then learn to support someone who is grieving. The closer someone is to a loss, the more support is needed. For instance, when a wife's husband dies, she is the one most in need of support. While her adult children will grieve, grandchildren will grieve, and friends will grieve, she is the one who spent the most time with him and will often feel the most pain. Support needs to be directed inward toward her. Who is next in the concentric circle? Perhaps the adult children, perhaps close friends. Sharing grief and supporting those nearest to the center of loss offers community and connection during a pivotal time. Connections within families and friendships can grow closer during this time, but they can also grow apart. This can happen when people are unable to process loss and grief or when they get caught up in ego-driven details. For example, in the case of death, family rifts often arise over the will or estate and how it's divided. Remember also that death is not the only loss we experience. Change, like when we switch jobs, move homes, get married, get divorced, or when children go off to college, can also feel like a loss. Some of these events might be joyful occasions, but they can also make you feel like a part of yourself is left behind. Giving a nod to these feelings is crucial; allow yourself to feel them, but don't get stuck in them.

Emotions, by their very nature, are fluid. We usually don't feel one emotion at the same level for a long time. There's an ebb and flow. The more you recognize that emotions are fleeting, the easier it will be to move through them with ease. You'll begin to see and feel that "this too shall pass" (a general axiom found in wisdom texts throughout the ages). This too, shall pass means realizing that whatever we feel in the moment will not last forever. Therefore, allow yourself to thoroughly enjoy laughter and joy because it won't always be around. Likewise, let yourself feel a loss as part of your delicate human journey, knowing you won't be stuck there forever. Good times will come back around.

We have only discussed laughter and grief here, but consider sharing any emotion you are feeling with someone dear to you. It's about you being able to name and express what's happening inside, "I'm frustrated today because things aren't going my way." Acknowledging your feelings in this way can help you avoid taking your frustration out on your loved ones. You are letting them know you have a big emotion inside, and if they notice this or feel it, they can be reassured that it's not about them. And if you notice big emotions in someone close to you, recognize the situation and try not to take it personally.

Rather, be curious and say something like, "You seem angry. Would you like to talk about it?" or more simply, "How are you feeling right now? I am here for you." Then, you can ground yourself and be a listening, compassionate ear for someone you care about. You don't have to fix anything. This is key to remember. A big part of connection and communication has to do with simple presence. It's about being there with someone in their strong emotion, whether it is joy, grief, or anger. If you can be relaxed and present, you are offering an unconditional kind of love, a warm container to hold the most vulnerable parts of another person. To have this kind of relationship, where it is safe to share your emotions, is wonderful. Not only will you feel a greater connection with this person, but both of you will move through difficult emotions with considerable ease.

Words

We have established that communication doesn't have to use words. We can connect through body language and presence in many nonverbal and emotional ways. And yet, words are considered our primary tool for conveying our thoughts and emotions. Some people are naturally inclined to use words to describe things or paint an emotional picture. I have enjoyed writing most of my life, whether it is journaling, writing poetry, short stories, or a book like this one. I've always found the written word powerful because it allows me space to put my thoughts down and read them. Then, if they don't make sense to me, I can reword or rephrase them.

Speaking is another skill that relies upon words. Some people have a knack for coming up with the right words on the spot to make a point or explain something. But others struggle to find the right words, whether they are speaking or writing. I've counseled people who label themselves "terrible communicators." Sometimes, this means the message they intend to convey isn't quite understood by others. Sometimes, it unintentionally creates complete misunderstandings. Alternatively, they might avoid challenging communications because they don't know how to handle them or what words to use. I've heard some people suggest that words don't matter and we should just accept whatever someone says without taking their words personally. While it is good to practice patience and understanding and, in doing so, not take things personally, we must not be complacent or flippant with our words. To be on a path of growth is to continually work on the key components of communication, one of which is the importance of using words effectively. Words do matter.

The Lie of Sticks and Stones

There's a childhood expression, "Sticks and stones can break my bones, but words can never hurt me." While part of me can understand the intent of this phrase, encouraging resilience in the face of verbal bullying, the fact is that we know words hurt us psychologically. You can receive a thousand compliments, but if one person insults you, chances are this is what you will remember.

This is especially true of children when their identities are forming. What they hear from the adults around them impacts them, and whether we're aware of it or not, it remains as an echo in the mind for the rest of their lives (sometimes a quiet echo, sometimes a loud voice). We are all impacted by the words spoken to us, particularly those from people we love.

The difficulty here is that sometimes we don't intend to hurt others, but because we aren't careful with our words or aware of the sensitivities of the person with whom we are communicating, we inadvertently cause harm. While awareness and more mindful communication can help prevent some of this, even the most skillful communicator's words will hurt someone. This is because we all see life through our own personal lenses, which are formed from our very individual circumstances and experiences. It's also because we all have emotions and sometimes react from a place of hurt within ourselves. We then end up uttering hurtful words.

Although others' words will likely hurt you, and your words will at some point hurt others, you can work toward excellence (not perfection because there's no such thing) in using your words. You can also practice grace and understanding in hearing and using words. If someone you love or even a stranger says something that hurts you, you might consider that it's not about you but is coming from a place of pain inside them. This is not meant as an excuse for bad behavior but rather as a framework to create understanding and lessen the impact of hearing harsh words. It's also a way you can forgive yourself if you misstep and say something hurtful. Of course, a sincere apology should be offered if you realize your words have caused pain, even if it was unintentional.

These days, there are lots of extreme judgments around words causing pain. Someone misspeaking out of ignorance (not knowing any better) may be labeled a "hater" or a "narcissist." Although, in some cases, someone might have intended to cause hurt, perhaps this person didn't have ill intent and simply hasn't learned better ways of communicating or was acting from a hurt knee-jerk emotion. Here are a few examples to consider. Someone with an authoritative parenting style, which means being nurturing and supportive yet setting firm boundaries and limits for children, may be misunderstood. Words such as "No," and "You can't stay out until midnight," can be labeled as "controlling" or "abusive" and misconstrued as hurtful. Or a husband telling his wife he doesn't like the outfit she's wearing or would prefer her hair a certain way might be seen as controlling. We must remember that all behaviors fall on a spectrum. There's a wide span between abuse and a well-meaning person simply offering an opinion we disagree with. Someone being insensitive with words doesn't necessarily signal abuse. If people who have been insensitive are made aware of the impact of their words and actively work toward improving their communication, they are not behaving in an abusive manner. Rather, they are acting like a human being who isn't perfect but is trying to improve.

Emotional and psychological abuse is when someone is consistently cruel with their words and actions and refuses to change or even acknowledge that they are doing anything wrong or hurtful. Suppose you feel constantly insulted, controlled, invalidated, lied to, or blackmailed, and the person is unwilling to hear about the pain they cause, apologize for it, or change their behavior. In that case, it's important to seek the help of a therapist and/or leave the relationship. We want our relationships to be positive, not negative connections.

It's also important to remember that communication goes two ways: there's a speaker and a listener. Both have a responsibility in processing an interaction. Words matter, and the following section will help create greater skill in being a better listener and speaker.

Communication is Input and Output

When training people to be better communicators, I'm often initially told, "I can't wait for you to teach me to say the right thing!" I smile because that's the last stage of communication. We must learn to be better listeners first. Communication involves both input, where we are receivers and translators of information, and output, where we are message senders. The input piece is an essential first step. Input or listening isn't just about listening to and gathering information from someone else; it also involves listening to and understanding ourselves. When you do this, your interactions are more likely to ring true because your mind, heart, body, and action are aligned. Without this alignment, you are more likely to have regrets, make mistakes, and say the wrong thing at the wrong time. So, continue to get to know yourself and understand yourself by checking in and asking yourself how you are doing and what you need.

Mind Traps

As you continue to become more aware of yourself and your communication style, it can be helpful to understand the concept of mind traps. Mind traps are your growth edges or things to be mindful of as you move throughout your day and, undoubtedly, when interacting with someone. Here are three possible mind traps:

- Habitual Styles of Thinking: We all have certain ways of processing information, be it with logic or emotion, overthinking, or knee-jerk decision-making. There's nothing bad or wrong with having a habitual way of thinking, and I'm not asking you to change who you are. After all, you've survived this long doing whatever you've been doing. I'm suggesting that you simply pay attention to it. Be reflective and notice your natural reactions to events and circumstances without being critical; be objective and curious. Is there a pattern to how you think about and handle certain things? If it is hard to step back and see clearly, assistance from a therapist or loved one can be helpful. If you fall into autopilot without awareness, you might not always be as skillful as you could be. Practicing cognitive flexibility, which means being able to interpret reality in various ways, will help you perceive the world more objectively.

Ask yourself what the worst-case scenario is. Sit with that. Then, ask what the best-case scenario is. Sit with that. Life usually falls between those two extremes, although we might occasionally experience a high or a low. Our mind does a good job of creating stories that we end up believing. As I've mentioned before, Mark Twain said it perfectly, "I've lived through some terrible things in my life, some of which actually happened." The more we notice our mind's habits, the more we can gain greater control over the story we tell ourselves (and the more successful we will be in hearing other's intentions more clearly).

- Negative Self Talk: We've discussed this before as well. We can be very mean to ourselves on the inside. That inner critic doesn't just harm us; it also impacts our interactions with others. We tell negative stories about what someone "must" think about us. We assume the worst. We beat ourselves up because we aren't doing everything perfectly right now. Negative self-talk is a habitual way of thinking, but it is worthy of being called out on its own because it's so pervasive and harmful. Simple awareness can help shift this as well. Catch yourself in self-criticism and self-doubt, label it as such, and let it go. Then, change the story to what you can say to yourself that is positive or just different.

- Assuming What Others Are Thinking: This is another habit that is worth calling attention to. I'm stating the obvious here, but we cannot possibly see inside another's mind. We can guess, and if it is someone with whom we are close, perhaps we might be right at times. But it is always best to assume that you don't know what others are thinking unless they tell you. It's also important to remember that nothing others do is because of you. Their actions come from their own habitual style of thinking, which is derived from their own experience, an experience much different from yours. The more you can see this, the more you can begin to have compassion for others because you can see they're stuck in their own habitual styles, just as you are in yours. And you're both just doing the best you can. No need to take anything personally.

Consider these mind traps before or while you communicate with someone. Although communication can never be perfect, if your intention is to engage with awareness and understanding, it is far more likely you'll have a connected, successful interaction and relationship.

Effective listening is also an important part of communication. Here are some practices to get you started on being a better listener.

Input

Silent Listening Exercise

This is a wonderful practice that I have used in small groups, with couples, and with families. Silent listening helps us to discover our tendencies to interrupt, to tell our own story, or to try to fix someone's problem. Here's how to do it.

1. Get yourself a willing participant. This might be your spouse, partner, friend, sibling, coworker, or family member.

2. Both participants think of one thing they are stressed about and one thing they look forward to or are grateful for.

3. Both take turns sharing their thoughts for an allotted time; 3-5 minutes is good. While one talks, the other just listens and supports with nonverbals such as head nodding, eye contact, and relaxed posture, and allows the speaker to say everything necessary. (Listeners don't verbally respond. Not now, not ever, in this exercise. They just listen and support with nonverbal communication.)

4. Speakers, think about how it feels to talk about something stressful as well as how it feels to share something positive.

5. Listeners, notice your internal process, your urge to interrupt, share, or fix.

6. Both participants internally observe their own thoughts, feelings, and body sensations when talking and listening.

7. After each person has shared and the other has listened and responded nonverbally to the other's stress or gratitude, they can answer these questions and discuss them together.

   - How did you feel when speaking during the exercise?
   - How did you feel when listening during the exercise?
   - Did you notice any mind-wandering? If so, what was the distraction?
   - What helped you to bring your attention back to the present?
   - Did your mind judge while listening? If so, how did "judging" feel in the body?
   - Were there times when you felt empathy? If so, how did this feel in the body?
   - How did your body feel right before speaking?
   - How did your body feel right after speaking?
   - What are you feeling right now?
   - How do you think mindful listening would change your interactions with others?

Keep in mind this is just an exercise. It isn't a model of how to communicate. Of course, we need to verbally respond to someone when interacting. It is natural to have a back-and-forth, like a game of tennis in which we serve and return. However, consider how interrupting someone impacts the conversation. If a thought gets redirected, and you don't return to that space, those words might never be shared. Injecting a little more silent listening into normal conversation might allow for insight and understanding that could otherwise be overlooked.

Reflective Listening

The next step is learning how to listen reflectively. This means offering a mirror for someone else to help them feel seen, heard, and understood. When you use this tool, people will immediately feel more connected to you. Here's an exercise for both the speaker and the listener. Make sure to switch roles after going through the whole process.

1. Once again, find a willing participant to practice with.

2. Both people think of one thing they are stressed about and one thing they look forward to. This could also just be something they want to express.

3. Listeners, you will not be in problem-solving mode. You will actively listen to understand, not offer solutions or opinions.

4. Speakers, try breathing before speaking to compose your thoughts. Start your sharing by using words like "I feel," or "My experience is," or "I am wondering." Speak about what your experience is. Try not to make assumptions about anyone else's thoughts or feelings (avoid statements like, "you don't..." or "you think that..."). Express yourself as clearly as you can. Take your time. It is okay to pause to collect your thoughts.

5. Listeners, reflect on what you're hearing by starting with the words, "I hear you saying..." Then, re-phrase or summarize what you think you heard.

6. Allow space for corrections and clarifications from the speaker or clarifying questions from the listener. Use these open-ended questions if you're not quite sure you understand what the speaker is trying to communicate:

- What do you mean by…
- How did you…
- In what ways…
- Tell me more about…
- What's it like…

Be patient and observant as they answer. If you're practicing this in real life, keep in mind that some people might not have been asked for detailed reflections before. The fact that you're interested in them and what they have to say may evoke scary feelings or wonderful feelings. If they are unable to answer your questions, you might affirm your interest in what they have to say, then ask them to think about it and share another time. This is a wonderful practice to help couples explore their vulnerabilities and strengthen their bonds. In a corporate setting, it can create a safe, productive space where employees feel heard and that their ideas matter and are appreciated. The more you practice this in comfortable circumstances with acquaintances, coworkers, and friends, the more it becomes second nature. As people notice your positive communication style, they might even begin practicing reflective listening because they learn by your example.

Listening skills are paramount when it comes to connection, so keep practicing. Listen with your mind, heart, eyes, ears, and whole body. Be present, absorb, feel, and process. Then, and only then, consider responding.

Output

Output refers to what you might traditionally think of as communication. You share your thoughts, feelings, energy, and words with another human being. Being able to explain ourselves is an amazing and beautiful gift. While it might be easy to have a casual conversation about things you enjoy, most people struggle with being able to share constructive feedback when telling someone they're not happy or that they want someone to do something differently. It's considered criticism, especially if delivered with harsh words or an irritated tone. So, how can you share your honest feelings?

How to Initiate Constructive Communication

1. First, consider the pause. If you are annoyed, irritated, or certainly if you are angry, it's best to wait until you feel calmer before approaching someone. You might be able to resolve an issue in your mind because it's about you and no one else. (It's not necessary to share every annoyance with everyone). A skillful pause can last two minutes or up to two days, but no longer than that.

2. State what you observe. Remember to be as clear and concise as possible. Begin with something like, "I see that.." or "I observe the situation this way..."

3. Next, state how it makes you feel. Say something to the effect of, "When that happens, I feel..." Make sure you're not turning it back on the other person. Don't say, "I feel...like you don't listen," or "I feel like you are being hurtful." Keep it as simple as possible. Say, "I feel hurt." Or "I don't feel understood." Try only to use "I" and not the word "you." It will help prevent the other person from feeling defensive.

4. Finally, offer your request. "Would you be willing to..." Ask the person to consider saying or doing something differently in the future. Remember that people can't go back and redo something that's already happened, but anyone can practice trying to be more skillful in the future. And if you are told, "No, I can't do that." Then, ask what they would be willing to do to improve this situation next time.

5. When you speak, remember to be honest and authentic, say what you need to say in as kind a way as possible, and only say something if it is necessary. By filtering your words so they are honest, kind, and necessary, you are engaging in constructive communication.

Constructive communication can help you stand up for yourself. Here's an example from a recent real-life situation:

I was leading a women's retreat, and we were staying in this beautiful old mansion. After our first night there, we discussed how poorly most of us slept because of the loud sounds from the heating system in the house. I went to the main office to explain our problem. I smiled at the woman and said, "Hello, we are really enjoying the manor house, except we had a poor night's sleep because the heating system was making loud noises all night. I feel exhausted. I'm wondering if someone can check the system to see if there's something wrong."

She told me, "That's just how those old houses and boiler heating systems are." I felt like no action was going to be taken. I restated, "I hear you that radiators can be loud to some degree. However, we can't sleep and are exhausted. Could you send a maintenance man over to check the system and talk to us?"

She pushed back again, telling me that she didn't think anything could be done about it. I remained calm and said, "I would feel better if we spoke to someone about the system. Are you willing to call him to see if he's able to come over? I'll wait." She finally said yes, and long story short, the maintenance man was able to drain the system and share some tips about how to heat the house and then shut the heaters down at night so things were quieter. I was able to be honest, kind and speak what was necessary, using the constructive communication model. And we got the problem solved! I had to cycle through different versions of the same conversation before action was taken, but that's okay. People don't always hear and respond how you want them to. That shouldn't mean you concede, avoid, or get angry. Just try again, patiently.

Tone

Sometimes, it just feels like someone is being combative, not in the words they say, but in *how* those words come out. We might not even label it as tone of voice, but we know the difference between a sincere apology and a sarcastic one. We know the difference between a polite request and an irritated demand, even if the same words are used. This is called tone.

We need to get familiar with our own vocal tone when speaking to others because it can significantly impact how our communication is perceived. This has been a real growth edge for me because I realize, thanks to very honest, close family members, that I sometimes sound irritated or impatient, and I don't even realize it. I sometimes chalk this up to the fact that I "wear my emotions," and if I feel stressed, I can come across as sounding annoyed. But that shouldn't be an excuse for continuing to use a tone of voice that's off-putting to people. And besides, I am not communicating effectively if my words and intentions aren't heard because people just respond to my perceived irritation. I believe life is about continuous growth, so listen if a loved one mentions your tone of voice. Try to be aware of your feelings before you speak. If you feel stressed or irritated, try giving yourself a pause. Take a deep breath and be mindful of how you respond to someone. Be aware not just of the words you're using but also of the tone with which you speak.

Other Tips for Constructive Communication

- Say "I agree" even if you don't agree with what the other person said. Say, "I agree that we need to talk about this." This offers a bridge for further conversation.

- Tell the person what you learned and what you heard. Even if you just say, "After listening, I've learned that this topic is important to you." Include a paraphrase of what you heard if you can, so they feel validated. Say, "That's helpful to know."

- Don't demand apologies. Apologies need to be authentic. You can create space for one by saying, "Can we talk about what happened?" You can share your feelings, but you can't ask the other person to apologize. A forced apology doesn't feel good anyway, for either the speaker or the listener.

- Once again, try not to take what someone else says personally. I know this is a tough one. When you start to feel upset about what someone has said, remember it's not usually about you but is very likely a reflection of their emotional state. Tell yourself, *Let it go; it's not about me.* With practice, this gets easier.

Useful Connection Resources

I realize that changing how you communicate might seem overwhelming or futile, especially if the other people in your life aren't also working on improving their communication style. Please remember that these are just tips and suggestions to consider over time. Punah punah. No one could implement all these practices simultaneously. Be gentle and patient with yourself and with others. Life is a long journey, and we can all work toward being a better version of ourselves tomorrow than we are today. This doesn't mean that today or yesterday, you were a terrible communicator or person. Most human beings are doing the best they can. That looks different for everyone on different days. Compassion is about recognizing that our level of effort and our "best" will differ depending on our circumstances, how much sleep we've gotten, and our emotional state. This leads me to offer some additional reading to help cultivate awareness and gentle understanding in the pursuit of personal growth.

The Four Agreements by Don Miguel Ruiz
This is an insightful book that offers four basic but challenging rules for living a happy life. And while I've touched on several of the concepts in this book, *The Four Agreements* is worth your time.

Nonviolent Communication: A Language of Life by Marshall Rosenberg
This book offers a method of communicating with others that is clear and kind. Although it is similar to what I've offered in this section, Rosenberg goes into greater depth and offers examples that can help you understand how to get comfortable with this style of communication.

The Five Love Languages: How to Express Heartfelt Commitment to Your Mate by Gary Chapman
If you don't know what love languages are, I highly recommend reading about them. Love languages refer to both how we feel love and how we give love. It is so important to know what makes your friends, family, and significant other feel loved.

In addition to these, there are many other excellent books on how to create more intimate, meaningful connections in your life through understanding and being a better communicator. Hopefully, some of these will help you on your journey.

Takeaways

As we come to the end of *The Space to Choose*, I hope you will reflect on the threads you have seen woven throughout Mindfulness, Discovery, Care, and Connection. I have very purposefully repeated myself, punah punah. While many of the ideas and quotations I've shared in various sections of this book are interconnected, the essence of all we have explored can be found in these three concepts:

Mindful awareness

Again and again, you can practice paying attention to what's in the present moment. Your body. Your breath. Your energy. Your emotions. Your thoughts. You can learn to see reality more clearly by taking a bird's eye view of whatever circumstances you're faced with. Then you can work toward finding equanimity in what is.

Perspective

Your opinion and judgment can often cloud your ability to see reality clearly. Being able to see other perspectives is vital on a path of action-oriented insight. If you practice equanimity in what you have control over and what you don't, you learn acceptance. And in acceptance, you can feel peace and choose a path forward.

Skilled action

The Space to Choose is ultimately about how you can take skilled action in your life. You can practice having intention and remembering your values and purpose as a guide. You can care for yourself deeply so that you can persevere through difficulties. You can learn how to skillfully express yourself and listen to others. In turn, you may live a happier, more purposeful life. It requires time and effort, as well as gentleness and patience. You won't always hit the mark, but it's the forward trajectory that will create your personal growth.

As one of my teachers, the wise Max Strom says, "If you start looking at your time as your lifespan, everything will change." His words have inspired me to contemplate how I choose to spend my life and to consider what fulfills me.

Now, I ask you, what are you spending your life on? Is it what you want or need? Is it what fulfills you? If not, then tomorrow's another day. Give yourself the space to choose the life you want, one moment at a time.

Notes

Introduction

1. This quote is commonly attributed to Viktor Frankl. However, it is author Stephen R. Covey who found this quote in a library book and thought it fitting to describe Frankl's views - but he did not note down the book's author and title. The quote is attributed to Frankl across various internet sources and publications. The website viktorfrankl.org explains further: https://www.viktorfrankl.org/quote_stimulus.html.

2. Chödrön, Pema. 2000. *When Things Fall Apart: Heart Advice for Difficult Times*. Shambhala Publications, 11.

Part One

3. This is an ancient story passed on from teacher to student. I first heard it from a teacher of mine. It can be found in various sources, as the original author is unknown. Here is one. l. Sean, Farmer. 2018. "Two Monks and a Woman — Zen Story." *Medium*, June 30. https://medium.com/@soninilucas/two-monks-and-a-woman-zen-story-c15294c394c1.

4. Pema says this phrase in many lectures and has written a whole book about this concept. The comments here are a paraphrase of the content in this book: Chödrön, Pema. 2010. *The Wisdom of No Escape: And the Path of Loving-Kindness*. Shambhala Publications.

5. Staaf-Sturgill, Joni. "Remember" is an unpublished poem.

6. This Christian poem is commonly attributed to Reinhold Niebuhr, though it is in the public domain and commonly cited in Alcoholics Anonymous.

7. Hölzel, B. K., Carmody, J., Vangel, M., Congleton, C., Yerramsetti, S. M., Gard, T., & Lazar, S. W. 2011. "Mindfulness Practice Leads to Increases in Regional Brain Gray Matter Density." *Psychiatry Research* 191 (1): 36–43. https://doi.org/10.1016/j.pscychresns.2010.08.006.

8. Staaf-Sturgill, Joni. or Staaf-Stamford, Joni. Recordings of Guided Body Scans are Available Online if You Search YouTube @Mindfulness With Joni and on the Insight Timer App under Joni Staaf Stamford (formerly Sturgill).

9. Achor, Shawn. 2010. *The Happiness Advantage: The Seven Principles of Positive Psychology That Fuel Success and Performance at Work*. New York: Broadway Books.

10. Achor, Shawn. 2010. *The Happiness Advantage: The Seven Principles of Positive Psychology That Fuel Success and Performance at Work*. New York: Broadway Books, 120 (Kindle edition).

Part Two

11. Mydans, Seth. 2022. "Thich Nhat Hanh: Quotes from a Zen Master." *The New York Times*, January 22. https://www.nytimes.com/2022/01/22/world/asia/thich-nhat-hanh-quotes.html.

12. Wallston, K. A., & Wallston, B. S. 2004. "Multidimensional Health Locus of Control Scale." *Encyclopedia of Health Psychology*, 171-172.

13. Frankl, Viktor E. 1962. *Man's Search for Meaning: An Introduction to Logotherapy*. Boston: Beacon Press, 76.

14. Frankl, Viktor E. 1962. *Man's Search for Meaning: An Introduction to Logotherapy*. Boston: Beacon Press, 75.

15. Hanh, Thich Nhat. 2014. *No Mud, No Lotus: The Art of Transforming Suffering*. Parallax Press, 13.

16. Mydans, Seth. 2022. "Thich Nhat Hanh: Quotes from a Zen Master." *The New York Times*, January 22. https://www.nytimes.com/2022/01/22/world/asia/thich-nhat-hanh-quotes.html.

17. "Parents Who Had Severe Trauma, Stresses in Childhood More Likely to Have Kids with Behavioral Health Problems." 2018. *ScienceDaily*, July 18. https://www.sciencedaily.com/releases/2018/07/180709101155.htm.

18. "Adverse Childhood Experiences (ACEs)." n.d. *Cleveland Clinic*. https://my.clevelandclinic.org/health/symptoms/24875-adverse-childhood-experiences-ace.

19. This is an exercise Steve Treu offers to his clients. He explores these kind of conversations in his book, Treu, Steve. 2016. *New Eyes: A Unifying Vision of Science and Spirituality*.

20. This quote was found in Ralph Waldo Emerson's journal in November 1842. https://www.walden.org/50-quotations-by-ralph-waldo-emerson/.

21. This quote and commentary can be found in this article: Rosenberg, Larry. n.d. "Shining the Light of Death on Life: Maranasati Meditation (Part II)." *BCBS*. https://www.buddhistinquiry.org/article/shining-the-light-of-death-on-life-maranasati-meditation-part-ii/.

Part Three

22. Prochaska, J. O., & DiClemente, C. C. 1983. "Stages and Processes of Self-Change of Smoking: Toward an Integrative Model of Change." *Journal of Consulting and Clinical Psychology* 51 (3): 390-395. http://dx.doi.org/10.1037/0022-006X.51.3.390.

23. Hansen, M., Jones, R., & Tocchini, K. 2017. "Shinrin-Yoku (Forest Bathing) and Nature Therapy: A State-of-the-Art Review." *International Journal of Environmental Research and Public Health* 14 (8): 851. https://doi.org/10.3390/ijerph14080851.

24. Allen, K., Kern, M. L., Rozek, C. S., McInerney, D. M., & Slavich, G. M. 2021. "Belonging: A Review of Conceptual Issues, an Integrative Framework, and Directions for Future Research." *Australian Journal of Psychology* 73 (1): 87–102. https://doi.org/10.1080/00049530.2021.1883409.

25. "What Are Sleep Deprivation and Deficiency?" 2022. *NHLBI, NIH*, March 24. https://www.nhlbi.nih.gov/health/sleep-deprivation.

26. Lasater, Judith Hanson. 2016. *Living Your Yoga: Finding the Spiritual in Everyday Life*. Shambhala Publications, 37.

27. Hölzel, B. K., Carmody, J., Vangel, M., Congleton, C., Yerramsetti, S. M., Gard, T., & Lazar, S. W. 2011. "Mindfulness Practice Leads to Increases in Regional Brain Gray Matter Density." *Psychiatry Research* 191 (1): 36–43. https://doi.org/10.1016/j.pscychresns.2010.08.006.

28. Journal, Elephant. 2022. "This Pema Chödrön Quote Perfectly Redefines Karma." *I'm Not "Spiritual." I Just Practice Being a Good Person*. Medium, October 13. https://medium.com/elephantspirituality/this-pema-ch%C3%B6dr%C3%B6n-quote-perfectly-redefines-karma-328108f81f60.

29. I read this story in Judith Lasater's *Living Your Yoga: Finding the Spiritual in Everyday Life*. Shambhala Publications. The story is from Dreiser, Theodore. 2023. *An American Tragedy*. Good Press.

30. Louie, D., Brook, K., & Frates, E. 2016. "The Laughter Prescription: A Tool for Lifestyle Medicine." *American Journal of Lifestyle Medicine* 10 (4): 262–267. https://doi.org/10.1177/1559827614550279.

31. Staaf-Sturgill, Joni. or Staaf-Stamford, Joni. Recordings of Guided Body Scans are Available Online if You Search YouTube @Mindfulness With Joni and on the Insight Timer App under Joni Staaf Stamford (formerly Sturgill).

Part Four

32. Wohlleben, Peter. 2017. *The Hidden Life of Trees: What They Feel, How They Communicate*. HarperCollins UK.

33. Holt-Lunstad, Julianne. 2021. "The Major Health Implications of Social Connection." *Current Directions in Psychological Science* 30: 251-259. https://doi.org/10.1177/0963721421999630.

34. Hölzel, B. K., Carmody, J., Vangel, M., Congleton, C., Yerramsetti, S. M., Gard, T., & Lazar, S. W. 2011. "Mindfulness Practice Leads to Increases in Regional Brain Gray Matter Density." *Psychiatry Research* 191 (1): 36–43. https://doi.org/10.1016/j.pscychresns.2010.08.006.

35. Escalante, A. "Science Discovers the Perfect Formula for Hugging." *Psychology Today*. https://www.psychologytoday.com/us/blog/shouldstorm/202006/science-discovers-the-perfect-formula-hugging. Posted June 24, 2020.

36. Roshi, Joan B.. 2020. "Purify Your Motivation." *Tricycle: The Buddhist Review*, November 10. https://tricycle.org/article/motivations-and-impact/.

Bibliography

Achor, Shawn. 2010. *The Happiness Advantage: The Seven Principles of Positive Psychology That Fuel Success and Performance at Work*. New York: Broadway Books.

Allen, David. 2011. *Getting Things Done: How to Achieve Stress-Free Productivity*. Hachette UK.

Allen, K., Kern, M. L., Rozek, C. S., McInerney, D. M., & Slavich, G. M. 2021. "Belonging: A Review of Conceptual Issues, an Integrative Framework, and Directions for Future Research." *Australian Journal of Psychology* 73 (1): 87–102. https://doi.org/10.1080/00049530.2021.1883409.

Chödrön, Pema. 2000. *When Things Fall Apart: Heart Advice for Difficult Times*. Shambhala Publications.

Chödrön, Pema. 2010. *The Wisdom of No Escape: And the Path of Loving-Kindness*. Shambhala Publications.

Dreiser, Theodore. 2023. *An American Tragedy*. Good Press.

Frankl, Viktor E. 1962. *Man's Search for Meaning: An Introduction to Logotherapy*. Boston: Beacon Press.

Gershon, Michael. 1998. *The Second Brain: The Scientific Basis of Gut Instinct and a Groundbreaking New Understanding of Nervous Disorders of the Stomach and Intestine*. Harper.

Gladwell, Malcolm. *Blink: The Power of Thinking Without Thinking*. Back Bay Books, 2007.

Hansen, M., Jones, R., & Tocchini, K. 2017. "Shinrin-Yoku (Forest Bathing) and Nature Therapy: A State-of-the-Art Review." *International Journal of Environmental Research and Public Health* 14 (8): 851. https://doi.org/10.3390/ijerph14080851.

Holt-Lunstad, Julianne. 2021. "The Major Health Implications of Social Connection." *Current Directions in Psychological Science* 30: 251-259. https://doi.org/10.1177/0963721421999630.

Hölzel, B. K., Carmody, J., Vangel, M., Congleton, C., Yerramsetti, S. M., Gard, T., & Lazar, S. W. 2011. "Mindfulness Practice Leads to Increases in Regional Brain Gray Matter Density." *Psychiatry Research* 191 (1): 36–43. https://doi.org/10.1016/j.pscychresns.2010.08.006.

Journal, Elephant. 2022. "This Pema Chödrön Quote Perfectly Redefines Karma." *I'm Not "Spiritual." I Just Practice Being a Good Person.* Medium, October 13. https://medium.com/elephantspirituality/this-pema-ch%C3%B6dr%C3%B6n-quote-perfectly-redefines-karma-328108f81f60.

Kabat-Zinn, Jon. 2009. *Wherever You Go, There You Are: Mindfulness Meditation in Everyday Life.* Hachette UK.

Louie, D., Brook, K., & Frates, E. 2016. "The Laughter Prescription: A Tool for Lifestyle Medicine." *American Journal of Lifestyle Medicine* 10 (4): 262–267. https://doi.org/10.1177/1559827614550279.

Lasater, Judith Hanson. 2016. *Living Your Yoga: Finding the Spiritual in Everyday Life.* Shambhala Publications.

Lasater, Judith Hanson. 2016. *Relax and Renew: Restful Yoga for Stressful Times.* Shambhala Publications.

Moeller, R. W., Seehuus, M., & Peisch, V. 2020. "Emotional Intelligence, Belongingness, and Mental Health in College Students." *Frontiers in Psychology* 11: 499794. https://doi.org/10.3389/fpsyg.2020.00093.

Prochaska, J. O., & DiClemente, C. C. 1983. "Stages and Processes of Self-Change of Smoking: Toward an Integrative Model of Change." *Journal of Consulting and Clinical Psychology* 51 (3): 390-395. http://dx.doi.org/10.1037/0022-006X.51.3.390.

Rosenberg, Larry. n.d. "Shining the Light of Death on Life: Maranasati Meditation (Part II)." BCBS. https://www.buddhistinquiry.org/article/shining-the-light-of-death-on-life-maranasati-meditation-part-ii/.

Rosenberg, Marshall B., and Deepak Chopra. 2015. *Nonviolent Communication: A Language of Life: Life-Changing Tools for Healthy Relationships.* PuddleDancer Press.

Roshi, Joan B., and Joan B. Roshi. 2020. "Purify Your Motivation." *Tricycle: The Buddhist Review*, November 10. https://tricycle.org/article/motivations-and-impact/.

Santos, Laurie. 2023. "Why Virtue is the Key to Your Happiness." *Bigthink.com*, October. https://bigthink.com/the-well/why-virtue-is-key-to-your-happiness/.

Sean, Farmer. 2018. "Two Monks and a Woman — Zen Story." *Medium*, June 30. https://medium.com/@soninilucas/two-monks-and-a-woman-zen-story-c15294c394c1.

Seligman, Martin E. P. *Flourish: A Visionary New Understanding of Happiness and Well-being.* Simon and Schuster, 2012.

Strom, Max. 2012. *A Life Worth Breathing: A Yoga Master's Handbook of Strength, Grace, and Healing.* Skyhorse Publishing, Inc.

Strom, Max. 2012. *There Is No App for Happiness: Finding Joy and Meaning in the Digital Age With Mindfulness, Breathwork, and Yoga.* Simon and Schuster, 2016.

Staaf-Sturgill, Joni. or Staaf-Stamford, Joni. Recordings of Guided Body Scans are Available Online if You Search YouTube @Mindfulness With Joni and on the Insight Timer App under Joni Staaf Stamford (formerly Sturgill).

"Suffering and The Second Arrow." 2009. *Spirituality, Therapy, and the Good Life*, August 27. https://tammiefowles.com/2009/08/27/suffering-and-the-second-arrow-2/.

Treu, Steve. 2016. *New Eyes: A Unifying Vision of Science and Spirituality.*

University of Texas at Austin. 2019. "Interacting with More People is Shown to Keep Older Adults More Active." *ScienceDaily*, February 20. Retrieved November 13, 2023 from www.sciencedaily.com/releases/2019/02/190220074610.htm.

Van Der Kolk, Bessel. 2014. *The Body Keeps the Score: Brain, Mind, and Body in the Healing of Trauma.* Penguin UK.

Wagner, Jerome P. *The Enneagram Spectrum of Personality Styles: An Introductory Guide.* Enneagram Studies and Applications, 1996.

Wohlleben, Peter. 2017. *The Hidden Life of Trees: What They Feel, How They Communicate.* HarperCollins UK.

"What Are Sleep Deprivation and Deficiency?" 2022. *NHLBI, NIH*, March 24. https://www.nhlbi.nih.gov/health/sleep-deprivation.

Made in the USA
Columbia, SC
25 April 2024